SO-BJF-109

TEACHING GUIDES

FOR 50
YOUNG
ADULT
NOVELS

Roberta Gail Shipley

Neal-Schuman Publishers, Inc.
New York   London

FEB   1998   ELMHURST COLLEGE LIBRARY

Published by Neal-Schuman Publishers, Inc.
100 Varick Street
New York, NY 10013

Copyright © 1995 by Roberta Gail Shipley

All rights reserved. Reproduction of this book, in
whole or in part, without written permission of the
publisher is prohibited.

Printed and bound in the United States of America.

Library of Congress Cataloging-in-Publication Data

Shipley, Roberta Gail.
    Teaching guides for 50 young adult novels / by Roberta Gail Shipley.
        p.   cm.
    Includes bibliographical references and index.
    ISBN 1-55570-193-0 (alk. paper)
        1. Young adult fiction, American--Study and teaching.
2. Young adults--United States--Books and reading.
3. Teenagers--United States--Books and reading. 4. Young
adults in literature. 5. Teenagers in literature. 6. Youth in literature. I. Title.
PS374.Y6S55 1995
813.009'9283'07--dc20   95-36534

CONTENTS

Appendix

INTRODUCTION

The novel has replaced the basal reader in the classroom. Students and teachers have grown weary of the stereotypical stories found in those readers. Gone are the days of the ditto sheets, filled with literal questions to answer. Increasing use of novels for both classroom instruction and supplemental reading provides opportunities to involve today's students in serious discussions of issues that pertain to them and their peers. Exposure to appealing novels such as those included in these guides can instill young adults with a lifelong love for reading as well as foster the development of fine-tuned thinking skills.

In order for today's young people to be successful, they must develop problem-solving skills and learn to think critically and creatively. Reading, thinking, questioning, and discussing are essential tools for success in our world.

Teaching Guides for 50 Young Adult Novels includes novels that are well written, lend themselves to discussion, and are relevant to today's teenagers. Several of the novels have won many awards and honors.

The main section of the *Guides* is arranged alphabetically by title. Material for each novel begins with a list of subjects, a summary, and comments to guide the teacher. Next, there can be up to three sections: "Vocabulary," "Discussion Questions and Writing Exercises," and "Research Questions." Vocabulary is listed only for novels that have a specialized set of terms, such as sailing terms in *The Voyage of the Frog* or aircraft terms in *Hatchet*. Discussion questions are presented sequentially to maximize thinking skills and thus should be used in the order presented. These are open-ended questions, so a variety of answers should be encouraged. Because the answers are not found in the text itself, no page numbers are provided. Writing exercises are denoted by an asterisk (*) preceding the question number. Research questions are provided for those books covering specific topics or issues. These questions provide an opportunity for teaching research skills in which students use nontraditional sources. Many of the answers can be found by interviewing policemen and social workers, reading magazines, and using CD-Rom encyclopedias, online databases, or the Internet. I urge teachers and school library media specialists to facilitate and encourage use of these alternative sources to better prepare students for lifelong learning.

I suggest the following steps to structure an effective program for using the *Guides:*

1. Introduce the novel to the students. This can be done by asking students what they think the novel is about from looking at the cover, the title, and the vocabulary list (if there is one).
2. Discuss the meaning of the vocabulary. *Do not* have students write out definitions!
3. Read the first chapter aloud to the students to help them get into the story.
4. Assign reading a chapter or two at a time. They can read it at home or aloud in class. (I found that having my students read aloud in class worked well.) If a recording of the novel on tape is available, you can also play it while the students read along silently. This especially helps less able readers.
5. Discuss the questions while reading or after finishing a chapter. Ask students to explain their answers or if they agree with what has just been said. There are no wrong answers. Allow time for students to reflect.
6. Assign one or more of the writing exercises to be done in class or at home. The writing exercises can also be used as oral discussion questions. Encourage students to express their feelings and opinions in their writing.
7. Research questions can be assigned during the study of the book or as an extension after reading has been completed. I let the students each choose one question they wish to answer. Students especially enjoy working on the research with a partner or in small groups.

After students have finished reading the book, you may wish to give them a ten-question multiple choice test on the book. Tests for all 50 of these books and for 200 others are found in *Tests for 250 Young Adult Novels* also published by Neal-Schuman Publishers.

The appendix provides biographical information about the authors, including their addresses. Students often enjoy discussing the relationship between an author's life and his/her novel. Having author addresses readily available facilitates letting students write them—yet another opportunity for developing language skills and involving students with literature.

ALEX, WHO WON HIS WAR
Chester Aaron

SUBJECTS: *war, World war II, sabotage, hero.*
SUMMARY: *Alex discovers the body of a spy and later learns that two German spies are holding two elderly ladies hostage. He must cooperate or they will be harmed. Alex and the women are eventually rescued.*
COMMENTS: *Alex learns through his ordeal that people can hold opposing views in a war and still have a human side. This book easily lends itself to a discussion of what a war can cause good people to do that they would not normally do and what makes a hero.*

VOCABULARY

Allied Powers
Nazis
Fascists
Axis Powers
USO
infantry
airborne
fatigues
saboteurs
reconnaissance
Luftwaffe
4 F

DISCUSSION QUESTIONS AND WRITING EXERCISES

1. When Alex gets rid of the wallet, he states that taking the wallet is a crime *if he is found out.* Do you agree? Explain.

2. The Tom Mix radio stories always end with ''Straight shooters always win. Lawbreakers always lose.'' Is this true? Explain.

3. Everyone considers Alex and Larry to be heroes for finding the dead body. What is a hero? Do you consider the boys to be heroes?

4. If you were in Alex's situation, would you tell the authorities about Rosie and Clara being hostages? Why?

5. Why did the Germans bring Alex inside and threaten him when he didn't even know they were there?

6. Imagine you are Alex. If you had to confide in one person about your secret, which person would you tell and why?

*7. Write out a plan to capture the saboteurs and save Rosie and Clara.

8. Why does Hans bring Alex a gift and why does he ask him to stay for a while?

9. Why does Alex have conflicting emotions concerning being with Hans?

10. Hans asks Alex if he or Oliver could kill a boy. Could you kill a child if you were a soldier? Explain.

11. If the war is lost but not over, why can't Hans ditch his mission? Why is duty so important if you've already lost?

12. Why did Hans tell where the bombs were planted? What about his "duty"?

13. Why would Alex get Hans his coat knowing a few minutes before that Hans was going to kill him?

14. Why did Larry tell Alex's secret?

*15. How did Larry change from the finding of the body to the capture of the spies? What caused the change?

*16. Write a newspaper account of the rescue of Alex, Rosie, and Clara and the capture of the spies.

17. When a war is over, captured prisoners are released. Why wasn't Hans released since his act of sabotage was part of his assignment in the German forces?

*18. Imagine you are Alex. What do you say when you meet Hans's wife and children?

RESEARCH QUESTIONS

1. Who were the Allied Powers in World War II?

2. Who were the Axis Powers in World War II?

3. Who were the Nazis?

4. What are Fascists?

5. What caused World War II?

6. What is the USO and what does it do?

7. What is the procedure for identifying a dead body?

8. How did people who stayed home help the war effort in World War II?

9. What was the Battle of the Bulge and how did it get its name?

10. Were any acts of sabotage done in America during World War II? What were they?

ALICE IN RAPTURE, SORT OF
Phyllis Reynolds Naylor

SUBJECTS: *boyfriends, dating, friendship, relationships.*
SUMMARY: *Alice believes she must have a boyfriend in junior high in order to be popular in high school. Alice and her girlfriends go through many experiences as they get their first boyfriends.*
COMMENTS: *My students enjoyed discussing aspects of dating, since they were just beginning to date themselves. We talked a lot about expectations and reality.*

DISCUSSION QUESTIONS AND WRITING EXERCISES

1. Do you agree with the statement that you have to have a boyfriend in junior high to be popular in high school? Explain.

2. How many times do you have to go out with someone before you stop being nervous?

3. How do you get a boy to ask you out?

4. What does a girl buy a 7th-grade boy for a birthday present? What rules do you follow when buying gifts for boys? What is not appropriate and why?

5. If your hair were messed up would you lie and avoid people or tell the truth? Why?

6. What do you do to get a kid to behave when you are babysitting?

7. How long does it take to get over a parent's death?

8. What does it mean to go steady as a 6th or 7th grader? How is it different from going steady in high school?

9. Why does Mark think it is okay to take the bra when he thinks it is Elizabeth's but not when it is Pamela's?

10. Elizabeth and Alice aren't talking to Tom and Patrick until Mark apologizes. Can you assume guys know what's wrong if you don't tell them? Why?

11. Is it okay to call a boy on the phone? Why?

12. What does the statement " 'Sorry' doesn't make it right" mean?

13. How old do you think you should be to date? Go steady? Explain.

14. Elizabeth is embarrassed to eat in front of boys. What are you embarrassed to do in front of the opposite sex and why?

*15. Imagine you are Dear Abby. Give advice to Pamela, Elizabeth, and Alice about boys.

16. What do you think about the statement, "If you lie beside a boy on the beach before nine in the evening, it's okay, but after nine it's a sin"?

17. Why can't good things last forever?

*18. Write in your diary about your dinner at the country club.

19. Forty years ago, girls put paper clips on their skirts to show how many times they had been kissed. What do people do today to show this?

*20. After the date at the country club, Alice realizes that she needs to like herself and learn what she thinks of herself and what she wants to be. Write out what you want to be and what kind of a person you are.

21. If you could ask your parents anything about dating, what would you ask and why?

AND THE OTHER, GOLD
Susan Wojciechowski

SUBJECTS: *friendship, school, relationships.*
SUMMARY: *Patty and Tracy have always been friends. Their relationship is threatened when Patty gets a boyfriend. Tracy finds new friends since Patty no longer has time for her. Patty eventually learns that friends are important.*
COMMENTS: *This book lends itself well to writing poems, letters, and papers on friendship. We spent a lot of time talking about the definition of real friends and why it is important to have them.*

DISCUSSION QUESTIONS AND WRITING EXERCISES

1. Patty wonders how a person can really know if she is pretty. How do you know?

*2. Patty has a list of four things a boy must be in order to be her boyfriend. Write out a list of criteria for what a person has to be to be your boy or girlfriend.

*3. Patty has goals for 8th grade. Write out your goals for this school year.

*4. Write a persuasive paper telling why you should or should not have a school uniform.

5. Patty tells Tracy to stay off the phone so she can get a call from Tim. Is Patty being a good friend to Tracy? Explain.

6. Why do you think Tracy doesn't want to talk to Patty anymore?

7. Why do some schools separate the boys from the girls?

8. Is it good to have only one friend? Explain.

9. Why is Patty upset that Tracy has other friends? Has Tracy done anything wrong? Explain.

10. Since Tracy has other friends, what should Patty do?

*11. Pretend you are Patty or Tracy and write in your diary how you feel about what's going on between the two of you.

12. Is Father Damian your typical priest? Explain.

13. What qualities do you look for in a friend?

14. Patty thinks about her ten-year friendship with Tracy. Why do you think they were such good friends all those years? What made their relationship special?

15. If you were Patty, would you tell Father Damian about the liquor in the restroom? Why?

16. Is it okay to take the "medicine" to help your throat knowing it includes liquor?

17. Explain the statement, "Make new friends but keep the old; one is silver and the other, gold."

*18. Write an article for your school newspaper about you and your best friend.

19. Think about your best friend. Tell how and when you knew that person was your best friend and not just a regular friend.

20. Why does Father Damian wear colorful hats?

21. Are friends important and do we need them? Explain.

ARE YOU IN THE HOUSE ALONE?
Richard Peck

SUBJECTS: *rape, legal system.*
SUMMARY: *Gail is raped by the son of one of the richest and most respected families in town. Gail has to cope with people who don't believe she was raped and with the way the legal system views rape.*
COMMENTS: *This book is excellent and should be used with students who can handle talking about this sensitive subject. How to go about changing the laws and attitudes toward rape and rape victims can be discussed.*

DISCUSSION QUESTIONS AND WRITING EXERCISES

1. Gail wonders if making love and being in love are the same. What is the difference?

2. Gail wonders if she dates Steve because her parents don't like him. Would you date a guy to spite your parents? Explain.

3. What would you do if you got silent phone calls when you babysat? Do you answer the phone when you babysit? Why?

*4. Write a poem for someone you like.

5. Why do people in small towns not accept newcomers?

6. Explain the statement that life's a drama, the world is the stage.

*7. Everyone loves Malevich's class. Write about a class you love and why.

8. Why does Gail refer to the townies as superior?

9. If you got an obscene note after all the phone calls, who would you go to for help and why?

10. Why does Gail's dad pretend he still has a job?

11. Why does Alison tell Gail the note never happened?

12. Why does the counselor think Gail and Alison made the note up?

13. If you were Gail, what would you say to Miss Venerable after she accused you of lying?

14. What would your parents do if they learned you had been raped and knew who did it?

15. Why does the policeman act as if Gail got what she deserved?

16. Is there any action that can be taken against a policeman for refusing to write down the name of the guilty party?

17. Why does the law protect the rapist instead of the victim?

18. Why will nothing be done about Phil Lawver because of who his family is?

19. Why do Gail's parents avoid talking about the rape with her?

20. Why does Phil send flowers to Gail and why doesn't Gail tell her parents who sent the flowers?

21. What does Ms. Malevich mean when she says that eventually Gail will stop looking for justice at every turn?

22. Alison knew all along the notes were from Phil. Why does she still defend him and say Gail is lying?

*23. Imagine you were fired by Mrs. Montgomery and write out in your diary how you feel.

24. If you don't tell who raped you and make it public, are you to blame when the guilty person rapes again? Explain.

*25. Pretend you are Alison. Write a letter to the Lawvers explaining what you know and persuading them to get help for Phil.

*26. Write a letter to your congressman trying to get the rape laws changed and the penalty made more severe.

27. Do you believe there is such a thing as rape? Why?

*28. Write out how Gail's life will be different from here on out.

29. Do you believe Phil knew what he did? Explain.

30. If your friend were raped, what would you say to comfort her?

31. If you were raped, would you be willing to testify in court or would you just drop it? Explain.

RESEARCH QUESTIONS

1. How can the laws on rape be changed?

2. Where can rape victims go for help?

3. How many women are raped each year in your city, state, country?

4. What percentage of women are raped by people they know?

5. How many rapists go to trial and are convicted?

6. What safety measures can be taken to prevent rape?

THE BRAVE
Robert Lipsyte

SUBJECTS: *boxing, Indians.*
SUMMARY: *Sonny leaves the reservation and ends up in New York City. After having run-ins with drug dealers and the police, he takes up with a policeman who is an ex-boxer. Together they turn Sonny into a good boxer and also help him to work off his anger about who he is.*
COMMENTS: *My boys who didn't like to read enjoyed this book because it is about boxing. This is an excellent book to use with minority students.* The Brave *lends itself well to discussions on belonging and finding out who you really are.*

DISCUSSION QUESTIONS AND WRITING EXERCISES

1. What is the monster in Sonny's throat?

2. Is there such a thing as an accidental punch to the groin?

3. Sonny says he doesn't have a chance in the first place of winning. Why does he think this?

4. Why does the bus driver assume Sonny has booze on him?

5. Why does Sonny think people hate Indians?

6. Why does Sonny want to leave the reservation?

7. Sonny leaves the reservation in order to be somebody. What makes a person a somebody and not a nobody?

8. Sonny hit a cop. Why does Brooks let him go?

9. The first rule of the Deuce is to trust no one. What could give someone this outlook on life?

10. Why won't Sonny turn in Stick and Doll? After all, he owes them nothing and has a counterfeit bill.

11. How does Jake know that Sonny is a Running Brave?

12. Jake says Running Braves get their strength from the people. Explain.

13. If the worst of being white and Indian is being too good to work hard and not thinking you are good enough, then what is the best of each world?

14. Brooks tells Sonny to take control of himself. What does he mean by this?

15. Why doesn't Sonny want to live with his mother?

16. Why doesn't Sonny's mother like the reservation?

17. If Brooks were not good enough to be a successful boxer, why was he willing to be a contender? Would you be? Explain.

18. Why does Martin change his attitude toward Sonny just because he learns he's a real Indian?

19. What does Jake mean when he tells Sonny to follow the Hawk?

*20. Martin wants to be a writer. Write about Sonny and Martin's capture of Stick.

21. Who do you believe turned in Sonny to the commission for being a pro and why?

22. How did Sonny know Stick was the one who shot Brooks?

23. Why can't you be chief if you've spilled blood?

24. How did Sonny know Doll would not help Stick get away from him?

25. Martin gives Sonny the name "The Tomahawk Kid." If you were a boxer, what name would you choose for yourself and why?

*26. Write out how Sonny has changed his attitude from the first time he met Brooks to the last fight.

27. Who taught Sonny the most about boxing—Johnson, Jake, or Brooks? Why?

*28. Compare and contrast Jake's views of his Indian heritage with that of Sonny's.

RESEARCH QUESTIONS

1. Research the history and culture of the Moscondaga Indians.

2. What are the Golden Gloves and when did they begin?

3. What are the rules of boxing?

4. How does one train to become a boxer?

5. Who is Muhammad Ali and why is he great?

6. Who is Joe Frazier and why is he great?

BUFFALO BRENDA
Jill Pinkwater

SUBJECTS: *mascots, school, buffalo, newspapers.*
SUMMARY: *Brenda gets a job on the school newspaper and writes articles that get the newspaper shut down. The newspaper staff then writes an underground paper where they expose many things, including the horse meat that is being served in the cafeteria. Brenda gets the students to raise money and sends for a real buffalo for their school mascot. The students learn to take care of the buffalo and hide it until a proper home is found.*
COMMENTS: *Buffalo Brenda is a very funny, entertaining story. I think all children wish they were Brenda or knew someone like her. The book lends itself well to discussions on censorship and responsibility. Students can spend much time writing newspaper articles about subjects they have investigated.*

DISCUSSION QUESTIONS AND WRITING EXERCISES

1. Brenda says time doesn't matter. In life, real bonds happen instantly. Do you agree? Explain.

2. Explain the statement, ''Prejudgment is the foundation of bigotry.''

3. If someone gave you a nickname having to do with your personality or life, what would it be and why?

4. If you were named according to what your parents were doing the week you were born, what would your name be and why?

5. Explain the statement, ''If you didn't know you were afraid, then you can't say you were afraid.'' Do you agree?

*6. Write out what your first day of junior high was like and how you felt. What were your fears? Did they come true?

7. What does Brenda mean when she says she is a citizen of the world?

8. Explain Brenda's statement, ''A teenager needs something to push against.'' Do you agree? Why?

9. Do you agree with the statement, ''Hardly anyone ever admires true uniqueness''? Explain.

10. What is the difference between celebrity and popularity?

11. Does freedom of the press pertain to high school papers? Why?

*12. Pretend you are a reporter. Write an article for your school paper about the benefits of eating horse meat vs. cow meat.

13. If you formed a new club at your school, what would it be and why?

14. What is a booster club and what does it do?

15. What kind of preparations do you think need to be made to take care of a bison?

16. Slick gives the illusion that he smokes and is dumb in order to be cool. What do students at your school pretend to do and be in order to appear cool?

17. Other than a library, where would you go to learn about bison?

18. If you were to find a place at your school to hide your school's mascot, where would it be and why?

*19. Write a letter to the Department of the Interior requesting information on adopting a bison.

20. Do you think the booster club's parents were right in supporting their kids when the buffalo arrived? Would yours? Explain.

21. Do you think it was okay or justified for Brenda's mom to spy on the group? Explain.

22. What would be a more reasonable punishment than expelling several hundred students?

23. Why is the bison considered a national symbol?

24. How would the bison make the football team win?

RESEARCH QUESTIONS

1. How does one go about adopting an animal from the Department of the Interior in Washington, D.C.?

2. Have there been any legal precedents concerning school papers and freedom of the press?

3. What do the constitution and laws say about freedom of speech?

4. In what countries is horse meat eaten?

5. What are the merits of eating horse vs. cow meat?

6. What is Zen and where did it originate?

7. What are the requirements for forming a club at your school?

8. What goes into a club constitution?

9. How much does it cost to ship a bison across the country?

10. What are the different animals the government has to give away?

A CANDIDATE FOR MURDER
Joan Lowery Nixon

SUBJECTS: *elections, politics, corruption.*
SUMMARY: *Cary, whose father is running for governor, overhears a conversation about a murder. As a result, her father's office is broken into and Cary's life is in danger.*
COMMENTS: *This book shows what a family has to go through if someone in it runs for office. How the election process works and corruption can be researched along with our beliefs about the democratic system. This is an excellent book to use during an election year.*

VOCABULARY

candidate
candidacy
candid
terrace
niche
status quo
eavesdropping
campaign manager
governor
protection
anonymous
politicians
impeach
evidence
favoritism
investigation
deceit
primaries
aftermath
cynicism
graft
expose
gubernatorial election
hardball
idealist
partisan
nomination

DISCUSSION QUESTIONS AND WRITING EXERCISES

1. How will Cary's life be different if her dad becomes governor?

2. Why do you think Cary was being followed?

3. If you were being followed, what would you do?

4. Why would Cary's dad hire Dexter as a butler and handyman when he can't do either well?

5. Why do people make crank calls?

6. The newspaper is supporting the other candidate and is attacking Cary's dad. How can they do this? Isn't the media supposed to be unbiased?

*7. Imagine you are Cary. Write out your reaction to seeing your dad in the political cartoon sitting on his oil wells.

8. Cary asks, "Does anybody care about the truth?" Is truth important in politics? Explain.

9. Why doesn't Cragmore want Cary's dad at the scene of the accident?

10. If you were an honest businessman, would you welcome an investigation? Why?

11. Should kids be required to agree with their parents politically?

12. Should Allie not be allowed to help with Mr. Amberson's campaign because of her own father's wishes? Why?

13. What would you do if you got another phone call from a woman saying someone wanted to hurt you?

14. If someone trashed your campaign office would it make you scared, quit the campaign, or determined to win? Why?

15. What purpose would trashing a campaign office serve?

*16. Suppose you were running for office. Write a campaign letter explaining your goals and why you should be elected governor.

17. Cary describes her father in one word: honest. If you described your mother or father in one word, what would it be and why?

18. If you didn't trust a campaign worker what would you do and why?

19. Who do you think planted the drugs in Justin's car and why?

20. Is it right to attack the family and children of a candidate in order to win? Why?

21. Do most people vote according to the facts and issues of the campaign or according to the wealth, family, and prestige of the candidate? Why?

22. Does the end justify the means in a political campaign? Explain.

23. After Cary comes in late from meeting with Sally Jo she is not allowed to leave the house day or night without an escort. Is this being unreasonable? Explain.

24. Why does Justin dump Cary?

25. Cary's dad tells Cary that once a politician is shown to be corrupt he can still have political support because he's in the right party. What does this say about people in general? With this attitude, do you still believe in the popular vote of the masses? Explain.

26. If you were arrested on a trumped-up drug charge because someone wanted to hurt your friend, would you play it safe and stay away from them or still hang around? Would you believe the papers over your friend? Why?

27. Why didn't Cary's dad tell her up front who Dexter really was? Was he right not to tell her? Explain.

*28. Write an ending to the story telling what happens to everyone including the current Governor Milco.

*29. Imagine you are Sally Jo. Write your exclusive newspaper article about the big story.

*30. Write out your view of politics.

31. Justin's dad says idealists think the impossible can happen whereas Cary's dad says idealists make the impossible happen. Which statement do you agree with and why?

32. What kind of person does it take to become a politician?

RESEARCH QUESTIONS

1. Explain the process a person goes through to become the governor of a state.

2. Has any government official been impeached in your state and if so, why?

3. What is the process for getting a crooked politician out of office other than losing an election?

4. How much money does it take to run for governor and what does it pay for?

5. What do campaign volunteers do?

6. What is the standard procedure for protecting candidates and their families?

7. What incidents have there been of the families of candidates being attacked physically or verbally during a campaign?

CANYONS
Gary Paulsen

SUBJECTS: *running, Indians, visions.*
SUMMARY: *Brennan likes to run. When he is out camping he finds a skull. After much research, he learns the skull belonged to an Indian boy who was killed on a raid. Brennan has visions about the Indian. He realizes the Indian is telling him to take his skull to a place that was sacred to the Indian. Brennan runs across the desert to take it there.*
COMMENTS: *This book is good for learning about the Apache way of life which is described in some detail. From following what Brennan does, students can learn how to do research without using an encyclopedia.*

VOCABULARY

raid
medicine place
ancient place
manhood
warrior
bluebellies
dry wash
spirits
sign
gully
poverty
canyon
bluff
dunes
cliffs
spring
boulders
stronghold
vaqueros
visions
pathologist
morgue
archives
marauding
arroyo
hostiles
butte
fissure

DISCUSSION QUESTIONS AND WRITING EXERCISES

1. Why do Indians get new names when they become men?

2. What does it mean to walk with your neck swollen?

3. Coyote Runs starts to prepare for the raid so he can be a man. What do boys in America today do to prepare to be men?

4. When Brennan runs he forgets everything else. What do you do that causes you to forget your troubles?

*5. Brennan says when he meets Halverson that that is the point at which his whole life changed. Write about an event that changed your life. Tell how it changed it.

6. Coyote Runs seeks advice from the spirits at the ancient place. Where do you go to get advice and who do you ask? Why?

7. Why do you think Coyote Runs asks the Spirits for help instead of asking one of the tribe?

8. Coyote Runs puts paint around his pony's eye so he could see at night and tobacco on his hooves so he would be swift. Tobacco was also put on the arrows. Why does he believe these things will work? How does he know this? What superstitions do we have today that would seem strange to others?

*9. Coyote Runs always describes himself and his surroundings using nature. For example, his long black hair shone like a raven's wing in the light. Write out a description of yourself using only things found in nature.

10. Why does Brennan's boss, Stoney, not respect anyone who is rich?

*11. Brennan asks who knows a story in order to get the little boys quiet. Pretend you are Brennan. Write a scary story to tell around the campfire.

12. Why does Brennan not tell anyone about the skull? Would you? Why?

13. If you knew keeping a skull you found was illegal, would you keep it anyway? Why?

14. Brennan asks his mother if crazy people know they are going crazy. What do you think and why?

15. While reading the articles Brennan comes to think the engine that drove the West was violence. Why?

16. Why do you think the four soldiers who killed Coyote Runs lied about how they killed him?

17. Did the army sanction Indian executions?

*18. Pretend you are Brennan. Write in your journal about visiting the morgue.

19. Do you believe a person's long-dead spirit can speak to a living person? Why?

20. Why does Brennan's mother yell for him to run when she is the one who called the police in the first place?

*21. Write an ending to the story about what happens when Brennan returns from the medicine ground.

*22. Write out all the ways in which the Apaches show themselves to be very clever and smart.

*23. Compare Coyote Runs to Brennan. How are they alike and how are they different? What similar experiences do they share?

*24. Write out how Brennan is different at the end of the story from how he is at the beginning.

RESEARCH QUESTIONS

1. What was the purpose of the ancient place and medicine place?

2. How do Indians receive their names?

3. How did the Apaches live and how did they carry out a raid?

4. Do Apaches today still use tobacco on their horses' hooves and arrows and paint circles on their ponies' eyes? Do they still believe in these old ways?

5. Is it illegal to remove or take old bones or a skull from the ground if you find them? What must you do legally? What process must a person go through in order to keep a skull?

6. What is the process that is followed in order to identify a skull?

7. What can be learned from a skull?

8. How many species of beetles are there?

9. Are there any recorded Indian battles in or around El Paso? How many and what is known about them?

10. What causes dreams?

COLLIDESCOPE
Grace Chetwin

SUBJECTS: *time and space travel, aliens, ecology.*
SUMMARY: *Two humans and an alien from three different time periods collide in time and space and must work together to defeat a bad alien and keep history from being changed.*
COMMENTS: *Ecology is easily discussed through the reading of this book. Different time periods are shown on earth from the time of the Indians with little or no pollution or destruction to the present. Comparisons of times and lifestyles can be made and solutions can be sought.*

VOCABULARY

alien
intergalactic
planetary
interior
instrumentation
frequencies
amidships
fore
aft
holographs
scanners
porthole
stasis
activate
eons
anaerobic
infinity
doomsday
binary code
sector
androids
clones
nanosecond
wampum
assimilation
teleportation

DISCUSSION QUESTIONS AND WRITING EXERCISES

1. Mr. Ho says there is always more than one way out of trouble. Give an example from your life that proves this.

2. Her mother thinks Frankie should dress femininely now that she is fifteen years old. Do you agree? Why?

*3. Describe the fireball and explosion as a primitive American Indian with no knowledge of technology would. Explain what it means and how it happened.

4. Frankie asks herself what one person can do in the face of overwhelming devastation. What can one person do today to save our planet?

*5. Write out what you believe the world will be like 100 years from now.

6. If you could visit any planet, which one would it be and why?

7. The Delaware boys went through rites and trials to prove their manhood. What do boys go through today to show they are men?

8. How do we know what we hear about the past is true since no one was there to see?

9. Is assimilation wrong? Why?

10. Is anything okay if it is in the name of progress? Explain.

11. If you were Frankie, would you confront your mom about telling everyone except you about her having a boyfriend? Why?

12. Since HAHN can go to the future and back, why doesn't he know how he altered the future by his crash?

13. Sky-Fire-Trail was named by the event of the fireball at his birth. What would you name a child born today or this week that would reflect a historical event or natural phenomenon?

14. Since HAHN is not supposed to change history, why did he take Sky-Fire-Trail into the future with him? Wouldn't his newfound knowledge change the future?

*15. Why would HAHN let Sky-Fire-Trail keep the silver blanket when he returned him to the shore? Imagine you are Sky-Fire-Trail. Explain the silver blanket and the translator band to your tribe.

*16. You are living in the 20th century. Explain to someone from an ancient civilization what a washing machine, radio, or some other piece of technology we have is for.

17. HAHN and Frankie discuss taking another's land. Is it right or wrong? Why? How have we as Americans done this? Give examples.

18. HAHN is acquiring emotions. If you could choose whether or not you had any, what would you choose and why?

*19. Compare and contrast the benefits and drawbacks of being emotional vs. being unemotional.

20. Frankie calls Sky-Fire-Trail stubborn because he can't see but one way to save his people. Who is more stubborn, Frankie or Sky-Fire-Trail? Why?

*21. Sky-Fire-Trail says mothers are to be honored and respected. Their word is law. Today, how do we see our mothers? How are they treated? Write an essay entitled "Mothers."

22. If you could have an Indian teach you some skill or craft, what would you choose and why?

23. If you were Frankie, would you have hit the infinity button? Explain.

24. If you could go anywhere in a space/time ship, where would you go and why?

25. Speculate on how history would have changed if HAHN had not been able to leave Frankie's time.

*26. Two thousand years later, Frankie, Sky-Fire-Trail, and HAHN meet again thanks to the time/space ship. Describe their meeting.

27. The author has the theme of conservation running through the story. What is she saying about it? Give examples of the theme.

RESEARCH QUESTIONS

1. What Indians used to live in the area where you live now and what names did they give to the different places?

2. What research has there been in the area of androids?

3. Has life been found on any other planet?

4. What spacecraft are sent out to explore and what have they found?

5. Has any research been done on time travel?

6. What is the philosophy behind Tae Kwon Do?

7. What was Greenpeace?

8. How have oil spills affected the environment?

9. How are the rain forests being destroyed?

10. What was the area you live in like 50 years ago, 200 years ago, and 500 years ago?

11. Which Indian civilizations are extinct today and why?

12. What happened in history the day you were born?

13. What has been going on in the area of artificial intelligence?

14. What is DNA engineering?

15. What is the culture and history of the Delaware Indians?

COVERUP
Jay Bennett

SUBJECT: *drinking and driving.*
SUMMARY: *On the way home from a party where there was drinking, Alden has an accident. He hits and kills a pedestrian and then covers it up. Brad, who is also in the car, is drunk but eventually recalls what happened. Alden's father, who is a judge, covers up the crime which is eventually exposed.*
COMMENTS: *The use of alcohol is rampant among today's youth. This story brings into focus for students that drinking has consequences. This is an excellent book for discussing why teens drink and how to say no to one's peers.*

DISCUSSION QUESTIONS AND WRITING EXERCISES

1. Why would Brad let Alden take him home knowing he was too drunk to drive and having already objected to it?

2. Do you think Brad really doesn't remember what happened on the way home?

3. Alden says they are the fun generation and all that matters is having fun. Do you agree with this philosophy? Explain. What does this statement tell you about Alden?

4. Brad asks himself what they are trying to prove, to find, by drinking so much. Why do you think they drink so much?

5. Is there a drinking problem in your school? How do you know?

6. What does Alden's father mean when he tells Brad, ''We must compromise and make adjustments to situations''? Are there times when you should never compromise? Explain. When is it okay to compromise? Give an example.

7. Brad's parents go to Hawaii and leave him alone for several weeks. Do you think this is okay? Why?

8. Why doesn't Brad go to the police with his suspicions when he finds the watch? Would you have?

9. Brad has known Alden his whole life, yet he asks himself how well he really knows him. Is it possible to be best friends with someone all your life and not really know them? Explain.

10. What does Alden mean when he says that we kill minds, hearts, and bodies and then put on masks and smile and bow to each other?

11. Why does Alden leave Brad on Wilson Lane to walk home?

12. Why does Brad allow Alden to control their friendship and make all the decisions?

13. Why does Alden finally tell Brad that he hit a man after having tried to cover it up?

*14. Pretend you are Brad. Write a letter to Alden's father explaining that Alden has a drinking problem.

15. Brad says people believe what they want to believe. Is this true? Give an example.

16. Brad wonders about truth. What is truth and can there be many different versions of it? Explain.

17. Alden's mother says his life will be ruined if he doesn't tell and his father says it will be ruined it he does tell. Who is right and why?

18. How do you think the judge was able to get everyone to lie and cover up the accident for him?

19. The judge thinks Paul Hansen was just a drunk bum so it was okay that he died. Are some lives more important than others? Explain.

*20. Write how you think the accident has changed Brad for the rest of his life.

21. Do you think Alden's father should have been sentenced? Explain.

*22. Imagine you are Alden's mother. Write a letter to Alden in prison to explain why you refused to be a part of the cover-up.

23. Do you think the judge could have done what he did if he had not been a judge? Explain.

24. Who do you think showed more courage, Alden's mother or the judge? Why?

25. Do you think Alden believes he did anything wrong? Why?

*26. Write an ending to the story telling how each person's life was eventually affected by the cover-up.

RESEARCH QUESTIONS

1. What effect does drinking have on a person?

2. How many people are killed annually by drunk drivers?

3. Do drunks really not remember what happens when they drink?

4. How many teenagers drink?

5. Why do teenagers get started and continue to drink?

6. How many homeless are in your city? State? Country?

7. Why do people become homeless?

8. Is there any corruption among government officials?

THE DEAD MAN IN INDIAN CREEK
Mary Downing Hahn

SUBJECTS: *murder, drugs, mystery.*
SUMMARY: *Matt and his friend discover a dead body in a creek. Later they discover Matt's mother helping her new boyfriend smuggle drugs. Matt swipes one of the dolls that is stuffed with drugs and has to get it to the police before his mother's boyfriend can catch him and kill him. Matt devises a trap that leads to the eventual catching of the criminals.*
COMMENTS: *This story is good for a discussion of ethics. Matt does not believe his mother has done anything wrong by stuffing dolls with drugs or accepting expensive gifts from the drug dealer.*

VOCABULARY

quarry
trespassing
murky
camouflage
dugout
excavation

DISCUSSION QUESTIONS AND WRITING EXERCISES

1. Why does Matt's mother remind him of being fat in front of Parker?

2. Is it okay to call your parents by their first names? Explain. Why does Parker call his mom, ''Pam''?

3. Would you accept expensive gifts from a boyfriend such as a TV or VCR? Explain.

4. Why doesn't Otis like Evans?

5. Why does Matt throw up in the police station?

6. Why does officer Scruggs not answer any of Parker's friendly questions?

*7. Pretend you are Fish. Write the newspaper account of the dead man in Indian Creek.

8. Why does Parker think Pam is in trouble?

9. Why does Parker think Matt's family is like the TV families such as the Brady Bunch?

10. Why does Evans think Matt and Parker are in Jennifer's house when he was in front and they went through the back door?

11. What does Pam see in Evans to want him as a boyfriend?

12. Why doesn't Jennifer ask her parents to help Matt and Parker?

13. Is it okay to endanger a six-year-old's life by having her carry drugs to a police station? Explain.

14. At the quarry, how can Evans tell Pam he's leaving her to go with Flynn yet say he did everything for her?

15. Why does Evans take Pam with him in the van and leave the boys and Flynn behind?

*16. Write an ending to the story for Pam, Evans, and Flynn telling what happens to them.

17. Why doesn't Parker understand that Pam has broken the law?

18. Does Pam love Parker? Back up your answer with facts from the story.

19. Why does Evans get involved with Flynn knowing the kind of man he is?

20. Are there any situations where it is justifiable to sell drugs? Explain.

RESEARCH QUESTIONS

1. What is the penalty for selling cocaine?

2. How many people are estimated to be selling cocaine in the United States?

3. What are the effects of cocaine on the body?

4. How many people die annually from using cocaine?

DIXIE STORMS
Barbara Hall

SUBJECTS: *rural life, divorce, family.*
SUMMARY: *Dutch's cousin, Norma, whom she has never met, comes to stay with her on the farm for a while. Norma is sophisticated and does not want to be there. The crops are failing due to lack of rain and everyone is uptight. Dutch's parents are divorced and she is having a hard time accepting her father's desire to date. Norma's parents are also getting a divorce. The two girls in the end learn to get along.*
COMMENTS: *Excellent book on what extended families are and what makes up a family.* Dixie Storms *shows the problems different family members can have in learning to cope with divorce.*

VOCABULARY

drought
repossessed
heat lightning
depression

DISCUSSION QUESTIONS AND WRITING EXERCISES

1. Is it harder to lose a parent by death or by divorce? Explain.

2. Do children with only one parent have more problems than those with two? Why?

3. Everyone in Dutch's family has an unusual name. Where did you get your name?

4. Dutch says once people get popular they are obligated to act like jerks. Have you found this to be true? Explain.

5. Aunt Macy says you can't hate blood kin but you can hate your spouse. Why?

6. Norma says you really ought to treat your life as if it were important because one day it might be. Do you agree? Why?

7. Norma says indifference is the only way to protect yourself from everything. Explain how this works.

*8. Norma teaches Dutch how to write in a diary. Write your own diary entry about what happened to you yesterday.

9. Why does Flood read Bodean's mail and not give him his mother's letters?

10. Why does Flood start coming in drunk a lot?

11. Why would Flood be glad the tractor was repossessed?

12. Papa says families stick together and Flood says family is forever. Is this true? Explain.

13. Norma told Dutch to ignore Ethan to get him to like her but it didn't work. How do you get someone to like you?

14. Bodean killed a sparrow with his BB gun at a church social. How old should a boy be before he gets a gun?

15. Why does Bodean take a gun to a church social? Isn't it illegal to do so?

16. Dutch thinks about what she would miss if she left her town for good. What thing would you miss the most if you left your town? What person would you miss the most? Explain.

17. Dutch and the waitress talk about belonging while waiting for Norma's bus. How does a person know where they belong and can you ever really know? Explain.

*18. Pretend you are Dutch. Write in your journal about seeing Becky again.

19. Why doesn't Bodean believe Becky is his mother?

*20. Write a letter to Norma telling her how you really feel about her.

21. Why did Becky and Flood's marriage fail and what could they have done to make it work?

22. Aunt Macy says you can't protect children from the world. What do you think? Explain. If you could protect children from the world, would you? Why?

23. Why does Dutch not like Lucy?

24. What made Flood stop running away from problems?

25. Flood says it isn't good to have too high expectations of people. Explain why.

*26. Ethan makes all these rules about going steady. Write out your rules for going steady.

27. What does Dutch mean by the dark side of love?

28. Is it worth it to have a relationship knowing it may not last? Why?

*29. Flood decides not to move away. He likes his town. Write down all the good things about where you live.

30. Dutch's papa plays Chinese checkers with her to get her to talk about what's bothering her. What do your parents do when they want to talk to you?

RESEARCH QUESTIONS

1. What percentage of farmers lose their land or machinery due to crop failure?

2. How often do farmers lose a crop due to drought or flood?

3. Why do people drink?

4. What percentage of people are divorced?

5. What is the law in your area concerning guns, children, and licenses?

DON'T LOOK BEHIND YOU
Lois Duncan

SUBJECTS: *Federal Witness Protection Program, mystery.*
SUMMARY: *When April's father testifies against the mob, her family has to go into the Witness Protection Program. April does not accept this and almost gets her family killed. April eventually is able to kill the Vampire, who is one of the men who is after her family.*
COMMENTS: *Many personal sacrifices are made by many people in order to get criminals put away. This book lends itself well to discussions of obligations and duties we have as citizens. Is it worth the sacrifice? Don't Look behind You is an excellent fast-paced mystery.*

VOCABULARY

FBI
agent
testimony
bodyguard
witness protection
tailed

DISCUSSION QUESTIONS AND WRITING EXERCISES

*1. April has to leave without saying good-bye to any of her friends. If you knew you were moving and had only one day to talk to everyone and do something, what would you do and how would you spend that day?

2. If April and her family are supposed to hide out in a motel, why would April think they would go to a fancy hotel and dine out and swim? Why would she pack dressy clothes?

3. April's father has been working secretly for the FBI. If you were approached by the FBI and asked to work for them secretly, would you? Why?

4. Why can't April's family call Lorelei and tell her where they are?

5. Max keeps April's father from reading a letter threatening his family so he won't back out of testifying. Is this ethical? Explain.

*6. April's family is extremely bored at the motel. Write out a game plan that would fill time and entertain the family with a variety of activities.

7. Jim doesn't trust April not to use the phone. Would you? Why?

8. Why is Jim a bodyguard when he has arthritis in his hands?

9. What two things about April's letter tell Mike Vamp where they are? Is it April's or Jim's fault that Jim is dead? Explain.

10. Why doesn't April's question get answered about how long they'll be in the Witness Protection Program?

11. If you had to be placed in the Witness Protection Program, where in the country could you go where no one would recognize you?

12. Jim is dead and attempts were made on April's family. She still wants to go home to Steve. What does this tell you about the kind of person April is?

13. April was forced to have her hair cut off. How would you go about disguising yourself?

14. April's mom was hurt that Lorelei refused to hide out with them. If your relatives went into the Witness Protection Program, would you volunteer to go with them and give up everything?

15. The girl sitting next to April on the plane asked lots of questions. How would you make her stop so you won't slip up?

*16. Pretend you are April's mother. Write out your thoughts upon entering your new home.

17. Why is April's mom so angry about not being able to publish her manuscript?

18. What hobby, sport, or activity are you known for that you would have to give up if you went into hiding?

19. Why do April and her mother think their new identities and situation are temporary?

20. How should April convince Abby that she is not the girl from the plane?

*21. April overhears the girls talking about her in the restroom at the movies. Write out in your diary a rebuttal to all the cruel things they said. How would you have handled the situation if you were April?

22. April's dad explains to her how he testified because he needed to feel as though he had achieved something. How could his family have made him feel successful?

*23. Pretend you are Jodi. What story are you going to tell Steve about April when you get back home?

24. Why is Larry angry about April going to Disney World? Does he have a right to be? Explain.

25. Should April have hung up on Larry? Why?

26. April drinks spiked punch at a party to loosen up. Why can't she do this without the liquor?

27. Should people with a secret past ever drink? Why?

28. Larry tries to make out with April saying he has a right to since they've gone out every night for a month. Does a guy ever have the right to assume this? Explain. Do girls owe guys just because they date? Explain.

29. Why does Lorelei change her mind and decide to move to Grove City?

30. Why does April finally understand reality and accept her situation while at Lorelei's condo?

*31. April is surprised at what Lorelei chooses to take with her on their trip. If you could only take two suitcases with you and everything else would be lost to you forever, what would you choose to pack and why?

32. Have you ever had the feeling you were being watched? How did you feel? What lets you know you are being watched?

33. If you were April, could you have killed someone who was trying to harm your family? Explain.

*34. Did the story have a happy ending because April was lucky or because she was clever? Back up your answer with facts.

*35. When April's family moves away from Grove City they appear to be well adjusted. How have the different family members changed from the beginning of the hiding out to the present?

36. If the family has learned any lesson from their experience what would it be?

37. Why is it important not to look at what you've left behind?

RESEARCH QUESTIONS

1. What is the Federal Witness Protection Program and how does it work?

2. How does one qualify for the Federal Witness Protection Program?

3. Has anyone ever gone back to his/her old life after entering the Federal Witness Protection Program?

4. What is the U.S. Marshall's Office and what does it do?

5. How successful is the Federal Witness Protection Program?

THE FACE ON THE MILK CARTON
Caroline B. Cooney

SUBJECT: *missing children.*
SUMMARY: *Janie sees her face on the milk carton while eating lunch at school. She tells Reeve, the boy next door, and together they search for answers to find out who Janie really is. The ending has a twist to it.*
COMMENTS: *Students have a wonderful time trying to guess what really happened to Janie and seeing who was right. There is a sequel to this book and a movie that covers both books.*

VOCABULARY

lactose
intolerance
hydroplane
daymare
insanity
cult
Hare Krishna
commune
debrainwash
adolescent trauma center

DISCUSSION QUESTIONS AND WRITING EXERCISES

1. Why does Janie's father want to keep her a little girl?

2. Janie wants to change her name. If you changed your name, what would it be and why?

3. Janie daydreams about driving and her future family. What do you daydream about?

4. What is it like to be compared to your supersmart older siblings?

5. Why do Reeve's parents feel it is okay to tell everything about Reeve to everybody else?

*6. Imagine you are Reeve. Write a letter to your parents telling them how you feel about their gossiping about you to others.

*7. Janie remembers the dress and the itchy collar. Write about your earliest memories.

8. Janie thinks she couldn't have been kidnapped because only bad people do such things and she doesn't know any bad people. What kind of people kidnap kids?

9. Why would Reeve's parents say he is dumb? Is it ever appropriate to let your child know you think he/she is dumb? What effect would saying it have on a child? Would it make you quit trying or work harder? Why?

10. How do you know you have not been kidnapped?

11. Why does Janie tell no one about having been kidnapped?

12. If you discovered your face on a missing-child poster, what would you do and how would you approach your parents about the subject?

13. Why would Reeve want to live in a flood plain?

14. Janie drinks milk. If you were allergic to something would you eat it anyway? Why?

15. Janie takes cake decorating with her mother. If you and your mother took a class together to become close what would the class be and why?

*16. Janie compares herself to her parents. Write out how you are like your parents and how you are different.

17. Why does Janie think she is going insane?

18. Why does Janie remember things now that she has never remembered before?

19. Janie asks to see her birth certificate. What other things could she look for that would prove she really belonged with the people who raised her?

20. Why can't Janie finish dialing the 800 number? Could you?

*21. Pretend you are Janie. Write in your diary your thoughts upon finding the white polka dot dress in the old trunk.

22. Why does Janie deliberately hurt her mother by saying she'd rather have a cheeseburger than her mother's pot roast?

*23. Janie doesn't like the honor roll breakfast of jelly donuts and juice. She doesn't think it is okay for the jazz band and sports teams to get more recognition than the honor students. Think about why society puts band and sports first. Write an editorial for the school paper stating your point of view.

24. Why is Janie jealous at first at learning about Hannah and her parents loving someone else?

25. How would you explain to someone like Hannah why there is economic inequality in the world?

26. Why do cults use brainwashing while Christian churches don't?

27. Why did Hannah leave the cult for a while?

*28. Pretend you are Hannah's mother. Compose a letter to convince Hannah to leave the cult and come home.

29. Why did Hannah's parents choose Janie over Hannah when they realized they could only have a relationship with one?

30. Was it right for Hannah's parents to attempt to snatch her from the cult? Why?

31. Why did Hannah kidnap Janie?

32. Janie thinks her mom and dad are her parents because they raised her and love her. What makes someone your parent?

33. Why does Janie go all the way to New Jersey and then not admit that these red-headed people are her family? Does she really want to know? Would you? Explain.

*34. You are at the Springs' house. Write out a speech you are going to memorize in order to introduce yourself to them.

35. Reeve says his parents will never believe that he and Janie didn't cut school to learn about sex. If you were Reeve, how would you convince your parents you didn't sleep with Janie?

36. Why don't Janie and Reeve call their parents to say they are okay?

37. Janie's mom says they love her and everything will be okay. Does love conquer all? Explain.

38. If you were raised by someone else you called Mom and Dad would you want your real parents to be a part of your life at all? Explain.

39. Why don't Janie and her father want to go to the Adolescent Trauma Center? Would you? Explain.

40. Janie feels she was a bad child because she gave up her family for a sundae. Is she being fair to herself? Explain.

41. Janie throws up thinking about New Jersey. Why?

42. Why does Reeve insist Janie tell her parents?

43. Is Reeve being fair when he says, "Tell your parents or you can't see me anymore"? Why?

44. After Janie and Reeve break up she realizes all that is important to anyone is being first in somebody's life. Is this true? Explain.

45. Reeve says it is no accident that Janie wrote and addressed a letter to the Springs. Why would she do this?

46. Janie says writing cleanses: it removes the badness from her mind and keeps it safely on the paper. Explain.

47. Is it right not to let your birth parents know you are alive?

48. Why does Janie's mother call the Springs? Would you have if you were Janie's mother?

49. How will Janie convince the Springs that she is Jenny?

*50. Write about Janie's first meeting with the Springs for the local paper.

*51. Tell how a year from now Janie's life will be different.

52. Is it reasonable to demand that the Springs not prosecute Hannah? Why?

53. As old as Janie is, do you think she will be forced to live with the Springs? Why?

RESEARCH QUESTIONS

1. How many people have lactose intolerance?

2. How do you get selected to be on a milk carton?

3. How many children have been found due to their pictures being on milk cartons?

4. What are the effects of lactose intolerance?

5. How many cults are there in the United States?

6. Why do people join cults?

7. History and beliefs of the Hare Krishna.

8. Why do people lose their memory?

9. What is the penalty for kidnapping?

A FAMILY APART

Joan Lowery Nixon

SUBJECTS: *orphan train, underground railroad.*
SUMMARY: *Frances's mother gives her children away to be placed in homes in the West. There are five books in this series which tells the stories of the six children who are adopted. This is the first book which covers the trip West on the train and Frances's story.*
COMMENTS: *Based on a true event in history, this story lets students see what rural America was like. This book is good for researching and comparing the beginnings of the adoption system with the present. Our students discussed why parents would give away all of their children.*

VOCABULARY

betters
balusters
balustrade
lamplighter
davenport
haberdasheries
stoops
gaslights
tenements
orphan
swell
urchins
sacrifice
abolitionists
diphtheria
underground railroad
bounty hunters

DISCUSSION QUESTIONS AND WRITING EXERCISES

1. Should you be ashamed of being poor? Why?

2. Why do people look down on the poor as though they were dirt?

3. Frances feels sorry for the orphans that get sent West. Are the orphans better off in New York City or in the West? Why?

4. Myra's aunt and uncle think she will die if she goes to the hospital. Why are people today afraid of hospitals?

5. Mike tells Frances that it's okay to steal if you would go hungry otherwise. Is this true? Explain.

*6. Pretend you are Frances. Write a letter to the man Mike stole from asking him to be lenient.

7. Do you agree with Mrs. Kelly's decision to give away all of her children? Explain.

8. Why do the farmers out West want to take in strange children from New York?

9. Mike saves Mr. Crandon's life when his shirt is on fire. Why is Mr. Crandon angry with him?

10. Frances puts out the brush fire with the men and boys of the train. What else might she be expected to do because she is dressed like a boy?

11. Was Mike wrong in picking the pocket of the outlaw on the train? Explain.

12. If you were Mike, would you have told the passengers you used to be a copper stealer? Why?

13. Frances has a hard time understanding sacrifice. Explain it to her. Give examples.

*14. Pretend you are Frances. Write a letter to one of the other children that would be encouraging. Tell about your own situation.

15. Would you be willing to give up a good job and move to help abolish slavery like Frances's new parents did? Explain.

*16. Write about a cause you would be willing to give up everything and start over for.

17. Frances has to change her ways so no one will know she is a girl. List the ways in which she must change other than her clothes.

*18. Johnny says Frances is a good storyteller. Write a story telling about the outlaws on the train.

*19. Frances learns to milk a cow. Write out step by step how to milk a cow.

*20. Write an essay for or against slavery.

21. Frances, her new parents, and Katherine Banks lie in order to save Frances when she is caught with the slave's scarf. Would you lie to save yourself or someone else? Explain.

22. Frances says she was not brave, just scared when she transported the runaway slaves to the Muellers. Can you be brave and afraid at the same time? Explain.

23. When everyone learns that Frances is a girl, she tells them she can still do the chores. After all she has done, why is Frances still afraid her new parents might not want her?

RESEARCH QUESTIONS

1. What was life like in Tomb Prison?

2. What was life like in New York City in 1864?

3. What was the Missouri Compromise?

4. What was the Fugitive Slave Act?

5. How did the Underground Railroad work?

6. What was the penalty for helping runaway slaves?

7. Trace the lives of some of the orphan train children.

8. How are orphans adopted today?

9. Who founded the first orphanage and where?

10. What was life like in the first orphanages?

11. How many slaves traveled to Canada on the Underground Railroad?

THE FIGHTING GROUND
Avi

SUBJECTS: *war, American Revolution.*
SUMMARY: *A young boy, Jonathan, answers the tolling of the bell and goes to war. In the 24 hours he is gone he is in a battle, captured, escapes, and learns that war is not glorious but terrible.*
COMMENTS: The Fighting Ground *can be read in a very short period of time and is an excellent book to be used to coincide with the study of the American Revolution in history classes.*

VOCABULARY

regiment
tyrannical
mercenary
allies
Hessians
Tories
traitors
tolled
flintlock musket
cartridge
powder horn
primed
strategies
tavern
militia
fife
grenadiers
bayonets

DISCUSSION QUESTIONS AND WRITING EXERCISES

*1. Write a paper comparing and contrasting the way a battle was fought in the American Revolution to how one is fought today.

2. Why does Jonathan want there to be a battle?

3. Jonathan's father is afraid of the war. What does he know that Jonathan does not know?

4. The bell at the tavern signals men to come to fight or that there is news. What is used today to signal a town that there is an emergency?

5. Why does the corporal lie about how many enemy soldiers are coming?

6. Why does Jonathan surrender instead of staying hidden behind the bushes? Did he do what a good soldier would do? Explain.

7. Why did the corporal keep his men in the dark about what was happening? Is it common practice today to keep the soldiers in ignorance? In what situations would this be preferable?

8. Why does Jonathan feel like a failure? Was he a failure as a soldier? Explain.

9. How would you communicate with someone who did not speak your language?

10. Why do the Hessian soldiers trust Jonathan?

11. Why doesn't Jonathan tell the Hessians about finding the little boy in the shed?

12. Why are the three Hessians indifferent to finding the boy's dead parents?

13. Why couldn't Jonathan kill the old soldier when he had the chance?

14. Why does Jonathan choose to help the Hessians against the Americans?

15. Why does the corporal speak to the Hessians in English telling them to surrender when he knows they don't understand English?

16. The corporal said the Hessians eventually would have killed Jonathan. Do you believe this? Why?

17. Why does Jonathan bust up his gun?

18. Why do most of the men not want to celebrate their victory with a drink at the tavern?

19. What was Jonathan spared from?

*20. Write how Jonathan's views of battle and war have changed from the first tolling of the bell to his return home to the farm.

*21. Write what Jonathan will tell his grandchildren about being captured by the Hessians.

22. Do you believe the three Hessians to be basically good or bad? Support your answer.

*23. Imagine you are Jonathan's father. Write out what is going through your mind about Jonathan being missing.

*24. Write a letter imploring the government to end the Revolution.

RESEARCH QUESTIONS

1. Why was the American Revolution fought?

2. Who were the Tories?

3. Who were the Hessians?

4. How did the British fight a war during the time of the American Revolution?

5. How many men were killed on each side during the American Revolution?

6. Who fought in the American Revolution besides the Americans and British?

7. What caused the American Revolution and how long did it last?

FLIGHT #116 IS DOWN
Caroline B. Cooney

SUBJECTS: *disasters, plane crash, rescue operations.*
SUMMARY: *A large plane crashes in Heidi's backyard while her parents are away on a trip. Heidi calls 911 and then begins to rescue the victims. Many of the rescuers who arrive to help are teenage EMTs. Many of the crash victims are saved through the courage of these teenagers.*
COMMENTS: *The story is gripping. Students learn from this book how one person can make a difference. This is an excellent book for research purposes. Students can research a disaster such as the bombing of the Federal Building in Oklahoma City to learn how a rescue operation works.*

VOCABULARY

EMT
paramedic
catastrophe
dispatcher
scanner
constables
jaws of life
the golden hour
triage
ravine
trauma
carnage
dry hydrant

DISCUSSION QUESTIONS AND WRITING EXERCISES

1. Heidi's house was named Dove House. If you named your house, what would you call it and why?

2. Do you think it is okay to send your children off to school where they only see their parents on holidays? Explain.

*3. Write a letter requesting an interview for an EMT job.

4. Daniel says Tuck has no personality. Is this possible? Explain.

5. Daniel blames everything that happens to him on the divorce. When is it time to take hold of your life and move on?

6. Do you think Daniel really wants Tuck to die in order to stop his father's wedding to Linda?

7. Darienne expects the woman to switch magazines with her. Why?

8. At first Heidi doesn't think the 911 operator believes her. Why?

9. Is it the job of the 911 dispatcher to decide if a call is a hoax? Explain.

*10. Patrick drinks coffee that he has to gag down because everyone he admires drinks coffee. Tell of a time when you did something you didn't want to do in order to be a part of the crowd.

11. Patrick had wished for a "really good" disaster. Why do you think someone would wish for something bad to happen?

39

*12. Imagine you are a newspaper reporter. Write up an article about the crash for the morning paper.

13. The doctor decided it was best to move people rapidly from the plane first and worry about head and spinal injuries second. Why?

14. Following the crash, the only able-bodied person who refused to help was Darienne. If you had been there and heard Darienne's refusal to help, what would you have done?

15. Ty gets stuck directing traffic. Of all the people on the scene, who has the most important job?

16. What does Heidi mean by her statement, "There is no such thing as time"?

17. Why does Patrick's mother say the Golden Hour is similar to the golden rule?

18. What does Patrick mean when he thinks to himself that he has seen only decency?

19. When overwhelmed, Heidi is told not to think about saving the world but saving one at a time. Explain.

20. Ty borrows a school bus. Is it okay to take something that does not belong to you in order to help someone? Where do you draw the line?

21. Why do you think Heidi's parents think she is so incompetent?

22. Why do you think Heidi is a disappointment to her parents?

*23. Carly has just died. Write out what you are going to say when you inform Carly's sister and family that she is dead.

24. Patrick doesn't think Heidi will ever become an EMT because she is rich. Only blue-collar people become EMTs and get their hands dirty. Is this stereotyping? Explain.

25. Patrick observes two men fighting about who is in charge. Why do you think they would do this instead of rescuing the victims?

26. Darienne lied during the TV interview about how much she helped. Are reporters responsible for airing untruths? Will anyone ever tell that the interview was not true? Why?

27. Ty lets Tuck drive the bus. What consequences can this have on Ty if the powers that be find out? Do you consider this irresponsible?

*28. How do you think the experience Heidi went through helping the victims will affect the rest of her life?

29. Heidi sees EMT volunteers as risk takers. What is a risk taker? Are you one?

RESEARCH QUESTIONS

1. Are volunteer fire and ambulance units as effective as paid ones?

2. What kind of training is needed to be an EMT?

3. Can teenagers be trained as EMTs?

4. What is the difference between a policeman and a constable? What kind of training does a constable have to have?

5. How many passengers can a 747 carry? What are the odds of being in a plane crash?

6. Can someone who refuses to help during a disaster be held legally or morally accountable? If so, what is the penalty?

7. What is the treatment for shock?

8. What is airline policy for notifying family and friends of crash victims?

THE GIFT OF THE GIRL WHO COULDN'T HEAR
Susan Shreve

SUBJECTS: *friendship, deafness.*
SUMMARY: *Eliza and Lucy have been friends for years. Lucy is deaf. Eliza wants to be in the school play but doesn't have the courage to sign up. Lucy signs both of them up. People are surprised. How can a deaf person try out for a musical production? Lucy teaches Eliza and the rest of the school about courage.*
COMMENTS: *Through Lucy students will learn to believe in and accept themselves whatever their limitations. This book is easily read in a short period of time.*

VOCABULARY

kewpie doll
insecurity
tryouts
orphan
musical
cruelty
depression
audition
humiliation
sarcasm

DISCUSSION QUESTIONS AND WRITING EXERCISES

1. Why does Eliza not like herself?

2. Why does Eliza think her mother had never had anything bad happen to her?

3. Why does Eliza think her mother knows nothing about life?

4. Describe Eliza's personality in chapter one.

5. Should Lucy be allowed to try out? Explain.

6. Can a person have too much personality? Explain.

7. How could Eliza understand Lucy when Lucy didn't talk?

*8. Have you ever had an experience where you could understand someone without their speaking? Write about it.

*9. Write about how you felt the first time you met a handicapped person. What was your first reaction?

10. Why are people cruel to handicapped people?

11. Do you agree with Lucy's mother that she should not learn sign language? Explain.

12. Eliza says she is the only one who ever tells Lucy the truth. Why would teachers and others not tell Lucy the truth about something?

13. Why would Lucy tell Eliza she has a wonderful voice when she has never heard Eliza sing?

14. Why does Lucy say she understands when she really doesn't?

15. Compare Lucy's attitude toward everything with Eliza's.

16. If the only way you could be famous was to be handicapped, would you want to be?

17. If you gave someone a gift that was not a physical, material gift, what would it be?

18. Eliza wonders how her life would be different if she had been born deaf. How would your life be different in such a situation?

*19. Practice being deaf for one day. Write about how you felt.

20. Pretend you are deaf and see how people treat you.

21. Why does Eliza not want to be around her friends anymore?

22. Eliza said her friends changed when they went into junior high. How have your friends and your life changed since you changed schools?

*23. Eliza's mother says Mr. Blake is truly unusual. He pretends to smoke and drink when he's with Eliza. Write about a person you think is truly unusual.

24. What does Mr. Blake mean by his statement that Lucy Bressler is the best teacher he's seen?

25. What does Eliza mean when she says, ''What I like best about my mother is that she listens to what I say and to what I really say''?

26. Why does Eliza pray that Louisa will be Annie?

27. Ever since Eliza was little she has wanted the lead in a musical. What is something you have wanted for years?

28. Why does everyone stand up and clap when Lucy finishes her audition?

29. Is it okay to try something you might not be good at? Explain.

RESEARCH QUESTIONS

1. How do deaf people learn to talk?

2. Demonstrate the deaf alphabet.

3. Why are some babies born deaf?

4. How do people read lips?

5. How can deaf people dance?

HATCHET
Gary Paulsen

SUBJECTS: *plane crash, survival, hope, problem solving.*
SUMMARY: *Brian goes to visit his father in Canada in a small plane. On the way the pilot has a heart attack and dies. Brian tries to land the plane. He then learns to live off the land making the same discoveries the Indians did. After several weeks he is rescued.*
COMMENTS: *Through this book students learn the importance of thinking for themselves and how to go about solving problems. Sequencing and brainstorming can be easily taught.*

VOCABULARY

bush plane
altitude
currents
horizon
rudder pedals
dashboard
copilot
controls
banked
turbulence
altimeter
transmitter
transmission
propeller
throttle
fuselage

DISCUSSION QUESTIONS AND WRITING EXERCISES

1. Brian's mother makes him wear a hokey hatchet on his belt. What have you ever been made to wear that you felt was hokey?

*2. Brian is terrified when he realizes he is alone 7,000 feet up in a plane. Write about a time you were truly terrified.

3. Why is there no parachute in the plane?

4. If you were Brian, would you have forced the plane to land or wait until you ran out of gas? Why?

*5. You are one of Brian's parents. Write in your journal about losing your son in a plane crash.

6. Brian realizes he needs water. What basic things do you need to survive and which is the most important? Explain.

7. Brian realizes he has never heard total silence before. Be completely quiet and tell what you hear.

8. Brian's old teacher says one should be positive and motivated. How can this help Brian?

9. Is Brian being realistic in thinking he will be found in a few days? Explain.

10. Brian thinks about the things he and Terry thought they would have if they were ever lost in the woods. If you could only have one thing with you, what would you want and why?

11. If you packed a survival bag, what would you put in it and why?

12. Why does the bear continue eating and not bother Brian?

*13. Imagine you are the bear. Tell your cubs about seeing Brian.

14. Brian believes his father and Terry were trying to tell him about fire in a dream. Do dreams have meanings? Explain.

*15. Write out step by step how to make fire the way Brian did it.

16. Why does Brian call the fire his friend?

17. What can the fire do for Brian?

18. Why does Brian forget about the searchers?

19. Brian has to keep hoping the searchers will come. Why is hope important?

20. Brian is beginning to see things differently. What is the difference between noticing something and seeing it?

21. Brian says his mind and body have come together and made a connection. Explain.

22. After Brian tried to kill himself with the hatchet he said the old Brian died and he was reborn a new Brian. Explain.

23. Why did Brian want to die and why did he later change his mind and want to live?

24. Brian calls his new hope "tough hope." Why? What is tough hope?

*25. Brian measures time by major events from his life in the woods. Write out a timeline of your life measured by meaningful events in your own life.

26. Why does Brian's first bite of meat taste better than anything he has ever eaten?

27. Why does the moose attack Brian?

28. Brian believes that if he can get the survival pack he will be rich. Why? What is your definition of rich?

29. Why is Brian surprised that the pilot's head has no skin on it?

*30. Write up a newspaper article on Brian and what happened to him.

*31. Pretend you are Brian. Write up your favorite memory from living in the woods.

*32. Write out a plan for Brian to enable him to survive the winter.

33. Would Brian have survived without the hatchet? Explain.

34. If Brian hadn't been rescued, what else would he have learned to do?

*35. Pretend you are Brian. Write a letter to your mother telling about flying the plane.

36. Pick a place such as the desert, ocean, forest, mountains, plains, etc., and tell how you would survive there.

*37. Did Brian survive because he was smart or because he was lucky? Back up your paper with examples.

38. How will what Brian has gone through and the knowledge he has gained affect the rest of his life?

39. If you were Brian, would you tell your dad the Secret? Why?

40. Why does Brian need to have a daily routine?

41. What discovery does Brian make about all the wild animals he encounters?

*42. Compare the Brian before the crash to the Brian after the rescue.

RESEARCH QUESTIONS

1. How do you perform CPR?

2. What are the emergency procedures when there is no pilot?

3. How do you land a plane?

4. How do you call for help on a plane?

5. What is the difference between airspeed and groundspeed?

6. What lives in the forest or woods where you live?

7. How long can you survive on water alone?

8. How are searches for downed planes done and when do they give up?

9. What is edible in the woods?

10. Research the following plants and animals: beaver, raspberries, choke cherries, hazelnut bushes, porcupine, black bear, snapping turtle, timber wolf, skunk, squirrel, moose, snowshoe rabbit, cottontail rabbit, ruffed grouse, bluegills, sunfish, perch.

INVITATION TO THE GAME
Monica Hughes

SUBJECTS: *space travel, survival, colonizing a new world, team work, welfare.*
SUMMARY: *Students who graduate from school have no jobs because the country's workers are mostly robots. Some of the students are invited to play a game. The game gets students ready to live on another planet but the students don't find this out until they wake up one day on another planet where they must draw on all their knowledge in order to survive.*
COMMENTS: *Ethics and the power the government should be allowed to have in controlling our lives are lively discussion topics. This book teaches students the importance of unity and working together in order to accomplish a goal or to stay alive.*

VOCABULARY

survival
scrounge
portcullis
cooperative
mesa
meteor
arid
meander
marshes
folk medicine
emigrate
diversity

DISCUSSION QUESTIONS AND WRITING EXERCISES

*1. Compare and contrast our 20th-century welfare system with that of Lisse's time. Which is preferable and why?

2. If you were unemployed and had no money, how would you spend your time?

3. Why are the thought police called that?

4. What really happened in the group's first visit to The Game?

5. Did the group find any clues? If so, what were they?

6. How did the group go about making each decision as to where they would go?

7. Why does everyone hate the unemployed when they are not unemployed by choice?

8. Why isn't the group allowed to bring anything back from The Game or take anything to The Game?

9. The Game manager was surprised a medic was not in their group. If Rich was supposed to be with them, what does this tell you about the planning of The Game by the government?

10. If the group really doesn't go anywhere because The Game is a computer-induced dream, why do they have to change clothes?

47

11. The newspaper talked of sterilizing the unemployed. Our own government has mentioned this with welfare women. Should this be allowed? Explain.

*12. Write out a plan to solve the population problem our world has today.

13. When the group needed a farmer and a doctor, Benta and Rich arrived. If you were to survive as pioneers in a new place, what skills would need to be represented in the people going and why?

*14. Pretend you are one of the group. Write out how you feel about realizing you are alone on a planet at the far end of the galaxy.

15. Give a name to the different animals the group found.

16. Why did the government not send any basic supplies with the group when they dropped them onto the planet?

17. What characteristics did this group have over other groups that made the government realize that they would survive?

18. What characteristics do pioneers need to survive and colonize a planet?

19. Why can't the government get rid of the robots since there is no longer a shortage of human workers?

20. Why didn't The Game manager just tell the group up front they were to colonize a new planet?

21. How did the group get ready for living on another planet? What kind of training would you need today to do so?

*22. Write a paper either defending or attacking sterilization of the unemployed.

*23. Write an advertisement describing the merits of Prize to get others to emigrate there.

RESEARCH QUESTIONS

1. Is space colonization viable today?

2. Has any research been done on colonizing another planet?

3. What types of folk medicine are practiced today?

4. Where does folk medicine come from?

5. What grows wild in your area that is edible?

6. What kind of population problem does the world have today and how is it being handled?

7. What problems are found in our welfare system and what is being done to correct them?

IS ANYBODY THERE?
Eve Bunting

SUBJECTS: *mystery, relationships, family.*
SUMMARY: *Marcus's mother rents the room over the garage to a man that Marcus doesn't like. When things start disappearing around the house, Marcus blames the man. Marcus eventually learns that the intruder is the man's son who ran away from his mother to go in search of his father. He had been hiding in Marcus's attic and stealing food at night. Christmas day brings the happy reunion between father and son.*
COMMENTS: *Problem solving can be incorporated by coming up with steps to solve this mystery. This novel highlights the needs of children from broken homes.*

DISCUSSION QUESTIONS AND WRITING EXERCISES

1. Why would Marcus's mother allow him to keep their house key on a nub in a tree instead of taking it to school with him? Is this wise? Why?

2. How can you tell that someone has been in your house?

3. Marcus is making his mom a bike for Christmas. If you made a present for your mom, what would it be?

*4. Marcus takes the blackthorn stick to bed with him. What do you do in your house to stay safe? Write out a safety plan for your home.

5. Why does Marcus dislike Nick?

6. Marcus and his mother put lights on the tree early but don't trim it until Christmas Eve. Then Marcus sleeps by the tree. What traditions do you have or would you like to have at your house?

*7. Write in your journal what you plan to say upon meeting your father for the first time in seven years.

8. Do you think Blake was smart or foolish in lying to his mom and in hitchhiking to find his dad? Why?

9. Is it wrong for a mother not to let her son know about or see his father? Explain and give examples.

10. How would you go about finding a missing parent?

11. Will Blake choose to live with his mother or his father? Why?

*12. Pretend you are Blake. Write a letter to your mom explaining where you are.

13. When Blake returns home, what questions will he have for his mom?

14. Marcus doesn't take the knife to the laundry room. He says he couldn't use it on anyone. Could you? Why?

15. Was Blake smart or lucky in finding his father? Explain.

RESEARCH QUESTIONS

1. How can you keep your home safe?

2. How many parents run away with their children and break their custody agreement?

3. What is the penalty for running away with your child?

4. Will a court tell you your parent's address if you ask?

THE ISLAND
Gary Paulsen

SUBJECTS: *nature studies, oneness.*
SUMMARY: *When Wil's parents move into a rural community, Wil discovers a small island on a lake. He goes out to the island and studies the animals there and tries to draw, imitate, and think like them. Eventually he starts camping on the island. The town, and especially his parents, don't understand his wanting to be alone out there. Wil learns a lot about himself and the animals and invites his father to join him on the island. His father begins to understand that Wil is special.*
COMMENTS: *The message of the story is that it is okay to be different and that not all learning comes from books. This is an excellent book to be read to coincide with studies the science classes are doing on observations.*

VOCABULARY

stern
compression
meditation
mandible
foraging
psychological

DISCUSSION QUESTIONS AND WRITING EXERCISES

1. Maypine is named after the pine forests. If you named your town according to what was in or around it, what would you call it?

2. Why does Wil's dad feel the need to pack up his family and move every year or two and change jobs?

3. Why does Wil's friend tell him moving is like slowly dying?

4. Why does Wil's dad attempt to fix the plumbing when in the past he has always failed at this job?

5. Why can't Wil describe Emil to his parents?

*6. Tell about a person you know who was almost too unusual to believe.

7. Why does Wil want to know the loons? If you picked an animal to study, what would it be and why?

8. Wil says his first day with the loons was long and strangely short. How can this be?

9. Wil's dad wants to have a berry farm. Is it better to enter into a lot of get-rich-quick schemes or work hard and save? Explain.

10. How is it that Wil can see himself in the heron?

*11. Compare your town to Pinewood.

12. Why do the farmers smile when talking about losing their farms?

13. Wil says life is like life. Others say life is like an Oreo. What do you say life is like and why?

14. Would you pay a plumber you had to spend all day cleaning up after? Why?

15. Why does Emil spit all over Wil's house?

*16. Wil writes about his grandmother after meditating. Write about your grandmother.

17. Wil wonders if he is too old to sit and watch ants. Why? Why are the ants interesting to Wil and other kids?

18. If Wil could ask the ants a question, what would it be and why?

*19. Pretend you are the loon at the lake. Tell your chicks about Wil.

20. Why does Wil say he is a part of the lake and the island? Explain.

21. Wil's dad, though very afraid, took his son up in a small plane for a birthday present. What are you afraid of that you would be willing to face for a friend and why?

22. When Wil tells Susan he is going to stay on the island, he says that if he leaves he will lose himself. What is he talking about?

23. What does Wil learn from watching the frog?

24. Wil is told by a teacher that you can paint or write better when you are a little bit hungry. Explain.

25. Why do Wil's parents think he is involved with a cult?

26. Is it unusual for a teenage boy to go camping in the summer alone? Explain.

27. What does Susan's father mean when he says Wil has the light on him?

28. Why do Susan's parents accept what Wil is doing when his parents don't?

29. Does Wil realize he is really drowning Ray? Explain.

30. Why does Ray beat up on people?

31. Why does Ray bring his two friends with him when he goes to the island?

32. How does the whole community know Wil is living on the island?

33. What is the difference between the turtle killing the fish and the heron killing the frog?

34. How is Wil like the turtle?

*35. Pretend you are Wil. Write a persuasive paper to convince your parents that you are okay and that you should stay on the island.

36. Wil decides you don't really learn a thing unless you become what you are trying to understand. How can you do this?

37. Wil remembers discussing dirty words at school. What makes a word dirty?

38. The counselor has to find a cure or treatment for Wil whose problem is that nothing is wrong. How do you do that?

*39. Pretend you are Wil. Write out a cure for what you think is wrong with the counselor.

40. Why does Wil's dad spy on him with binoculars?

41. Why does Wil invite his dad to join him on the island?

42. Why is Wil's dad about to cry when he accepts Wil's invitation to go to the island?

*43. How is Wil's life changed because of his island experience?

*44. Pick an animal and for a week really study it and then write about it and draw it.

45. What makes Wil's father finally understand Wil?

46. How has Wil changed and grown from the beginning to the end?

47. In the end was it a mistake for Wil to be interviewed by Anne? Explain.

RESEARCH QUESTIONS

1. How did your town get its name?

2. Research the following animals: loon, blue heron, waxwings, snapping turtle, sunfish, frog, ant.

3. Research your family tree.

4. How do ants communicate?

5. How do you mix colors to create new ones for watercolor painting?

LOSING JOE'S PLACE
Gordon Korman

SUBJECTS: *roommates, responsibility, adventure, budgets.*
SUMMARY: *Three high school students, Jason and two of his friends, rent Joe's place for the summer. They get jobs and learn to manage money and be responsible. Throughout the summer they run into colorful characters and have unique adventures, in the end causing Joe to lose his lease.*
COMMENTS: *This book can easily tie in with a math or economics unit on budgets. Budgets, cost of living, salaries, and percentages can be covered while reading this humorous book.*

DISCUSSION QUESTIONS AND WRITING EXERCISES

*1. Write a persuasive paper to convince your parents to let you stay in the big city with a friend all summer being only sixteen years old.

*2. The boys spend way too much money their first day in Toronto. Think about what expenses they will have. Come up with a budget for them.

*3. Jason and his friends describe their neighbors and give them names. Write a paper describing the neighbors where you live and give them descriptive names.

4. Does Ferguson realize he's done anything wrong when he ends up getting Don and Jason fired? Why?

5. Don says that girls say they want nice guys but they never do. Do you agree? Explain.

6. Why doesn't Jason tell Rootbeer to leave?

7. Why aren't Rootbeer's ribs broken when he is hit by the 2 x 4?

8. Do you think Jason would have thrown Rootbeer's body in a vacant field to keep from losing Joe's apartment? Why?

9. Why are the ambulance attendants angry that Rootbeer is alive?

10. Why does Jason think Don and Ferguson won't believe him about how Rootbeer got the grocery money?

11. How can Rootbeer be relaxing from executive burnout when he's never been an executive?

12. Rootbeer has 36 blank photos but likes the first one best. Explain.

13. Jason realizes he is thinking and acting like his mother when it comes to cleaning and bugs. Why is he cleaning the apartment when he won't clean his room at home?

14. Why does Jessica drop Don for Ferguson?

15. Of the four boys—Jason, Don, Ferguson, and Rootbeer—who makes the best roommate and why? Who makes the worst and why?

16. Why doesn't Mr. Plotnick really want Jason and Don to eat at the Pop Bistro?

17. Why don't the police believe Jason's story about the stolen car?

18. Rootbeer thinks a holding tank is relaxing. Where do you go to relax and why?

19. Name three jobs you think Rootbeer would enjoy.

20. What suggestions would you make to Plotnick to increase his business?

21. Why doesn't Don believe the man when he says Kiki doesn't live there?

22. What should Jason have done to solve his problem with the police taking his Camaro?

23. Does Jason have the right to change Plotnick's Deli without his permission? Why?

24. Why do the customers like Rootbeer's entertainment?

25. Why does Rootbeer carry a bunch of junk under his poncho?

26. Why does Plotnick become partners with Hamish when he can't stand him?

*27. Compare and contrast the Olympian Delicatessen with Chocolate Memories.

*28. Did the boys survive the summer because they were lucky or because they were smart? Back up your answer with several facts.

29. What was the most interesting event of the summer in your opinion and why?

*30. Of the four boys—Jason, Don, Ferguson, and Rootbeer—who do you identify with the most and why?

*31. Summer is over. Write a paper for school on how you spent your summer in Toronto.

RESEARCH QUESTIONS

1. What are renter's rights?

2. Where do renters go for help?

3. What are landlords required to do?

4. Pick any company in the United States and write to find out how much money was saved through automation and how many jobs were lost.

5. What is the penalty for making harassing phone calls?

6. What are the rules for getting into the *Guinness Book of World Records?*

THE MIND TRAP
G. Clifton Wisler

SUBJECTS: *mind control, telepathy, science fiction, space travel.*
SUMMARY: *Scott, who comes from another planet, is in an accident and goes to a hospital where the doctor in charge does mind control experiments. Scott has the ability to read minds and move objects. The doctor soon learns of this. The doctor has children in the hospital perform for him in order to learn of their abilities. Scott helps the children who want to leave escape and finds homes for them.*
COMMENTS: *This is an excellent book for discussing how far a scientist can go in the name of science. It also lends itself well to having students set up their own experiments, observing the results, and keeping a written record.*

VOCABULARY

observer
seer
earthers
investigators
telepathy
implant
transmit
receptive
mentalist
channel
healer
reconstitute
teleport
mentor
premonition
ESP
amplifier
precognitive
telekinesis
parapsychic
zeta waves
empathy

DISCUSSION QUESTIONS AND WRITING EXERCISES

1. Knowing that he is supposed to be dead, do you think Scott should have returned to earth for a visit? Explain.

2. Scott is supposed to blend in with everyone and act normally. Yet he fixed his broken body. Why?

3. Why do you think the hospital doesn't let anyone write letters or call home?

4. Gigi says all nine kids have ESP. Do all people in real life have some sort of ESP? Explain.

5. Is it right to have experiments done on you just because you are different? Explain.

6. Would you allow someone to put a microchip in your head? Why?

7. Do you think ESP is real or a hoax? Explain.

8. What kind of family would give up their children for experiments?

9. Why wasn't Scott taken to a regular hospital? Is this normal police procedure?

10. Why is reception bad at the institute but out of it the kids can read each other's minds easily?

11. How does Scott explain being able to read the hieroglyphics at the museum?

12. Why does Gigi think Scott was around when the hieroglyphics were originally written?

13. Why do you think Dr. Edgefield doesn't see anything wrong with holding Scott captive?

14. Why does Dr. Edgefield replace the glass windows with plastic ones?

15. How come Scott still can't escape once he's on the outside wall of the shower room?

16. Why can't Scott just black out the whole building and escape?

17. Who is more afraid of publicity, Dr. Edgefield or Scott? Why?

18. Tim was killed and cut up so the government could study his physiology. Is it okay to kill a person for scientific purposes if they are not human? Why?

19. Why does Dr. Edgefield let Scott see the files on the subjects of the past?

*20. Pretend you are Dr. Edgefield. Write up the file on Scott.

21. Since Scott can move objects, why can't he telekinetically remove the ring from the clamps and put it in his hand while he and the others are in the lab?

22. Do you believe aliens who look like humans could live among us and not be discovered? Why?

23. If Scott could put thoughts in George's mind to make him sleep, why didn't he do that to everyone and then just walk out?

24. The colonists won't let Tiaf and Scott stay with them because they are seers and they blame the seers for the destruction of their world. How can it be the fault of the seers?

*25. Pretend you are a TV reporter. Write an article about the fire at the institute.

*26. Pretend you are Dr. Edgefield. Write the government to ask for funding for your work.

*27. Pretend you are Danny and David and have just learned your daddy is an alien. Put your thoughts in a diary.

RESEARCH QUESTIONS

1. Is there such a thing as ESP?

2. How many people are thought to have ESP in some form?

3. Is there any research being done today on ESP, telepathy, or telekinetics? If so where and what kind is being done?

4. How many UFO sightings have been confirmed in the United States?

THE MONSTER GARDEN
Vivien Alcock

SUBJECTS: *monsters, science experiments.*
SUMMARY: *Frankie's brother brings home some goo from his father's lab and gives half to Frankie. Her goo grows into a monster she names Monnie. As she takes care of Monnie she begins to love it like a mother would. She hides Monnie and eventually finds a home for her where no one will want to cut her up in the name of science.*
COMMENTS: *The skills of observation and recording can be easily taught using this story.*

VOCABULARY

chauvinist
genetic
laboratory
transparent
petri dish
incubator
microscope
corrosive
sterilized
molecular biologist

DISCUSSION QUESTIONS AND WRITING EXERCISES

1. Do girls have smaller brains than boys? Explain.

2. Why is it okay for David to stay out longer just because he is a boy? Should the same rules apply whether you are a girl or a boy? Why?

3. What would you feed a monster?

4. If all of your older siblings were brilliant, do you feel you would have to compete with them or be just what you want to be? Explain.

5. Do you believe women can be anything or have any career a man can have? Should women be discouraged from certain fields? Explain.

6. If you grew a monster, who would you trust to go to for help?

7. Where would you hide a monster?

8. Why is Frankie no longer afraid of her monster or want to give him away?

9. Why was David so sure his goo was dead?

10. Frankie says it is too late for her dad to get to know her. Why?

*11. Write a descriptive paper on what Monnie looks like.

*12. Keep a scientific journal for one week on a plant, animal, or baby telling how it is changing.

13. Now that Monnie is so big, do you think the laboratory would hurt him? Explain.

14. Frankie can't take care of Monnie adequately now that it needs a pond to swim in. What should she do?

15. Is it better to tell an adult about Monnie and trust them or go on your own knowing Monnie is not getting good care with you? Why?

16. Does Monnie choose its own shape by looking at Frankie or does it just happen to have five fingers per hand now?

17. How do you know Monnie is intelligent? Be specific.

18. Even though Monnie started from goo it is alive. Does a living creature have the right to life? Explain.

19. The boys throw rocks at Monnie when it is asleep under the tree because they are afraid. Is it okay to hurt or destroy something because you don't understand it? What should you do?

20. Why is Frankie so protective of Monnie?

21. What does everyone think is the reason Frankie went to Didon?

22. How does Frankie's view of her father change from the beginning of the book to the end?

23. Why doesn't anyone ask Frankie for an explanation after she is rescued?

24. Frankie says it is easier to forgive your enemies than those who pretend to be your friends. Why?

25. Frankie pretends she is not hurt when the other students call her ''Frankenstein'' at school. Why do students call each other names? What would you do if people continually called you an unflattering name?

26. How has the experience Frankie had with Monnie changed her life?

*27. Pretend you are the boys who attacked Monnie. Describe to a reporter what happened.

RESEARCH QUESTIONS

1. What is a genetic engineer and what does he/she do?

2. What is a molecular biologist and what does he/she do?

3. What kind of genetic research is being done today?

THE MONUMENT
Gary Paulsen

SUBJECTS: *monuments, honoring men killed in action.*
SUMMARY: *Mick comes to town to design a monument to honor the memory of the men killed in previous wars. While there, he gets to know the town and its people. In doing so he comes up with an idea for the monument that surprises the whole town.*
COMMENTS: *This unit can be done in conjunction with the art teacher as students design their own monuments. Research can be done as students study past monuments that have been erected and the history behind them.*

VOCABULARY

monument
orphan
orphanage
adopted
grain elevator
community-minded
memorial
gnome
pervert
art

DISCUSSION QUESTIONS AND WRITING EXERCISES

*1. Write in your diary about what you thought when you saw Mick for the first time.

2. What does Mick mean when he says "life is organic"?

3. Why would living with a drunk couple be preferable to an orphanage?

4. What is meant by Mick's statement that Rocky is thirteen going on 50?

5. Would you have sneaked into the sheriff's backyard and stolen a dog? Explain.

6. Design your own monument.

7. Why do people make fun of the handicapped?

8. Why do the farmers always reach out and let the grain run through their fingers?

9. Rocky learns all the local gossip at the grain office. Where would you go in your town to hear all the gossip?

*10. If you wrote the local gossip column for the paper, what would you write? Write out a sample column.

11. Do you think it is a waste of money to have a monument? Explain.

12. Rocky goes to the town meeting because Fred and Emma decided she needed to be community-minded. What does it mean to be community-minded? Do you think it is important?

13. What stipulations or guidelines should be made before work on a monument begins?

14. Why should one have a monument built for a controversial war?

15. Who should design the monument?

16. Why does Python like Mick?

17. What makes something or someone beautiful?

18. Why does Rocky say Sister Gene Autry is beautiful when before she thought of her as ugly?

19. Why does Mick draw everything in town?

20. How would you capture the soul of a town?

21. What does Mick mean by "there's seeing and there's seeing"?

22. What is meant by the statement, "You are an artist. That can't be taught"?

23. Why do Mick and Rocky cry when they draw?

24. What can Mick learn from the cemetery?

25. Would you go into a bar knowing you would get beaten up?

26. How far would you go in the name of art?

27. Why do the people rip the drawings down?

28. Why do you suppose Mick put the pictures up?

*29. Pretend you are a reporter. Write an article for the local paper about what happened at the meeting.

30. What does Mick mean when he says, "Sometimes monuments don't seem to be monuments but are, just the same"?

*31. Write a poem to go on a plaque commemorating the dead.

32. Do you consider planting trees, a flower bed, or gardens art?

33. Mick drew the town in order to know it. What would he draw in order to know your town?

34. If someone drew a picture to get to know you, what would they see in the picture?

*35. Write an editorial for the paper discussing the opening day ceremony of the new monument.

RESEARCH QUESTIONS

1. What percentage of handicapped children get adopted?

2. What does "floor is open to discussion" mean? How do you run a meeting?

3. How much did it cost to build the Vietnam War Memorial in Washington, D.C.?

4. From the first discussion to completion how long did the Washington wall take?

5. Research Edgar Degas.

6. Research unusual monuments.

7. What has your town, city, state done to remember war deaths?

8. What kinds of war monuments are there in America?

9. How do other countries remember their war dead?

MOUSE RAP
Walter Dean Myers

SUBJECTS: *gangsters, hidden treasure, rap.*
SUMMARY: *Mouse and his friends search for money hidden by gangsters many years ago. Along the way, they talk with old gangsters and learn to work together resulting in their finding the money.*
COMMENTS: Mouse Rap *is a book to read just for the pure pleasure of reading a good book. It is funny and students love it. They also enjoy getting to write and perform their own raps.*

DISCUSSION QUESTIONS AND WRITING EXERCISES

1. Mouse's friends call themselves The Selects. If you and your friends came up with a group name, what would it be and why?

*2. Write in your journal about being beaten in basketball by a monkey.

*3. Mouse prefers to speak in rap. Write out your own rap.

4. Why don't Mouse and the boys want to dance with The Selects?

5. Mouse doesn't want to fight Bobby but thinks he will look bad if he walks out. What should he do?

6. If you were Mouse, would you fight for your rep? When do you think it is okay to fight? When is it okay to walk away?

7. Why does Mouse play ball with the monkey a second time knowing he lost the first time?

8. How come Mouse is happy to lose the second time when he was embarrassed the first time?

9. Why does Mouse assume Styx is gay? Can you assume that without being told? Explain. What is really wrong with Styx?

10. Why doesn't Gramps like Booster?

*11. If you found a million dollars and could keep it, what would you do with it?

12. Do you think Mouse should give his dad a second chance, considering how he left them before? Explain.

13. Why does Mouse think Buster will get him killed eventually when Buster scared off the mugger with a gun?

14. Why would Beverly ask Styx to be her girlfriend if she was already going with Mouse?

*15. Write in your journal about the fight on the basketball court with the guy with the artificial leg.

16. Explain the statement, "Sometimes things you want in life come with little price tags on them that read 'risk' and 'not sure' and 'confusion.'"

*17. Pretend you are a reporter. Write up the incident in the bank.

ONE FAT SUMMER
Robert Lipsyte

SUBJECTS: *being overweight, bullies, summer jobs.*
SUMMARY: *Bob gets a job taking care of Dr. Kahn's huge lawn all summer. A bully wants the job and continues to threaten Bob. Bob refuses to quit. As Bob works on the lawn he finds himself too tired to eat. By the end of the summer he has lost his fat and has stood up to the bully.*
COMMENTS: *Bob learned to like himself by the end of the summer. He learned that liking himself had nothing to do with his appearance. Students today need to learn that they are okay.* One Fat Summer *helps students learn to believe in themselves and deal with difficult people.*

DISCUSSION QUESTIONS AND WRITING EXERCISES

1. What is the difference between being conceited and being convinced?

2. Why does Dr. Kahn make a crack about Bob's weight when he hires him?

3. Why does Dr. Kahn cheat Bob out of his pay?

4. What should Bob have done when his pay was lowered to $.50?

5. Why is Bob unwilling to tell his parents about his summer job?

6. Why does Pete make a big show of taking Bob home that first day?

7. Why does Bob's father have no faith in him?

8. Joanie doesn't like her nose and Bob doesn't like his fat. What is the one thing you would change about yourself if you could and why?

*9. The Rumson boys want to mess with Bob. Imagine you are his best friend and write him a letter advising him on how to deal with the situation.

10. Bob thinks that to be accepted as a "regular" guy you have to like baseball and know the players and their averages. What do you have to do or know today to prove you are a "regular" guy?

11. Why doesn't Bob eat as much when he gets home from work as he used to?

12. Why does Bob go back to work on Monday after Willie threatens him to get him to quit his job? Would you? Why?

13. The grocer says black ball players can't be trusted. If you don't say anything when someone makes a racist remark, is it the same as agreeing with the statement? Explain.

14. Bob says the night spent on the island was not all bad. What good came out of his being stranded?

*15. Bob's father doesn't want his wife to work. Both Bob and Michelle are in high school. Write a paper either for or against mothers working.

16. Why does Bob feel Joanie is not the same person since her nose job and find it hard to talk to her?

17. Bob eats when he is happy and when he is sad. Why do people eat too much?

18. Bob's parents griped because he was fat and now that he's losing weight his mother doesn't like it and tries to get him to eat cake. She thinks he will gain his weight back. Why?

19. Michelle's and Pete's fathers blame each other's kids for sleeping together. Who's fault is it and why?

20. Why does Pete feel it is necessary to jump Willie and Jim when they are leaving?

21. Why doesn't Bob want a ride home with Pete after he almost drowns Willie?

*22. Write out what makes a real man.

*23. Write a letter to your dad explaining to him how you feel about being put down by him all the time.

*24. Compare and contrast Bob at the beginning of the summer with him at the end. Include more than just the weight change.

25. What would be a good project for Bob to write about at the end of the summer?

26. How would the story be different if Bob had quit the job with Dr. Kahn because of Jim's warning?

27. Several people at Rumson Lake are prejudiced. What makes people that way?

PILLOW OF CLOUDS
Marc Talbert

SUBJECTS: *divorce, suicide.*
SUMMARY: *Chester's parents get a divorce and make Chester decide who he wants to live with. He spends the summer with his father in New Mexico and decides that he wants to stay with him. Yet he believes it is his duty to live with his mother because she needs him. His mother attempts to kill herself. Chester's father explains that it is not Chester's fault. In the end Chester stays with his father.*
COMMENTS: *This book is excellent for teaching compare/contrast skills. Divorce and suicide are very relevant subjects for students today. Students need to learn not to blame themselves for situations that are out of their control. I enjoyed this book a lot.*

VOCABULARY

rut
irrigation ditch
gallery opening
depression
fiesta
arroyo
low rider
adobe
pinion nuts

DISCUSSION QUESTIONS AND WRITING EXERCISES

1. Why is it hard to say good-bye?

2. Chester thinks a lot about dying. Is this normal for teenagers? Why do people think about death?

3. Do young people think they are going to die? Explain.

4. Chester says his mother hurts the people closest to her. Do most people do this?

*5. Write about a time when someone close to you hurt you.

6. When Chester's parents get divorced, they make him choose who he wants to live with. No matter who he chooses, one parent will be disappointed. Is it fair to make a child choose? Explain. Could you do it?

*7. Chester tries to write a poem to remember Santa Fe by when he leaves. Pretend you are leaving the town and home you like. Write a poem to remember it by.

8. Chester goes to a place on the hill to be alone. Where is your place to be alone? Why is it special to you?

9. If you had to choose between two parents, would you choose the one you wanted to live with or the one who needed you? Why?

10. If you told your mother you were going to live with your father, would you put it in a letter, call, or tell her face-to-face? Why?

11. Chester hasn't been able to write poetry all summer. He says he has to be withdrawn and sad. Why is this?

12. Why do Arturo and Jose use wisecracks when speaking to each other? How do you know what kind of relationship they have?

13. Describe the kind of life Chester had with his mother.

14. What does the way Chester, his dad, and Florence respond when they think the hummingbird is dead tell you about them?

15. When Florence asks Chester to answer three questions about where he is happy, do you think she is trying to influence him to stay? Explain.

16. Chester is not sure if his thoughts and emotions are in agreement. What does he feel and what does he think?

17. Think of a time when your mind told you one thing and your heart said another. Which did you listen to?

18. When Chester sees a cat jump over a wall, he wonders how the cat knew there weren't rose bushes with thorns or broken glass on the other side. How do you think it knows, or does it?

*19. Write a paper comparing and contrasting Clifton, Iowa, to Santa Fe, New Mexico.

20. Do you think Chester made the correct choice when he chose to stay with his father and Florence? Support your answer.

21. Why does Chester's mom build a pool and want to buy him a computer? Are her reasons pure? Is what she is doing acceptable? Explain.

22. Chester thinks that praying is more for the person who is praying than for God, whoever He is. What does he mean by this statement?

23. Clifton resents his mother's rearranging and decorating his room and giving away his clothes. How important is privacy in your own room? How would you make your parents understand that your place needs to be truly yours?

24. Why does Chester try to look at his town through Jose's eyes?

25. Chester keeps saying over and over the old rhyme, ''Step on a crack, break your mother's back,'' as he gets angrier and angrier. Why is he angry and does he have a right to be? Explain.

26. Chester said his mom used to think it was funny when Chester drank too much. Should parents allow or encourage their children to drink? Why?

*27. Chester's mother read all of Chester's poems. Pretend you are Chester. Write a journal entry explaining what happened and how you felt.

*28. The people of Santa Fe dump trash and large objects into the arroyo. Pretend you are an environmentalist. What steps would you take to stop this practice? Write a letter to the city council concerning this problem.

29. When Chester shows the dirty magazines to Jose, he learns Jose doesn't share his enthusiasm for looking at them. Why doesn't Jose want to see them?

30. Chester keeps having the same dream about himself and his mother. Why does he keep having it?

31. Do you believe the people really feel better and get rid of their bad feelings when Zozobra is burned? Explain.

*32. Pretend you are Chester. Write a letter to your mother describing the burning of Zozobra. Be descriptive.

33. Chester asks Florence the difference between art and pornography. What is the difference?

34. Jose is afraid to show anyone his drawing. Chester doesn't share his poetry. Why are people afraid to be different and show what is special about themselves?

35. When people talk, Jose looks at their mouth and Chester looks at their eyes. What do you look at and why?

36. Why does Chester blame his mother's suicide attempt on everyone but his mother?

37. When Arturo finds Chester in his low-rider, he tells him that when life slaps you around, you slap back and don't run away. How can Chester fight back?

38. Chester receives a letter from his mother postmarked the day after her suicide attempt. If you were Chester, would you open the letter or throw it away? Why?

39. Chester doesn't know what to say to his mother after her attempted suicide. Write out what you would say to her if you were Chester.

40. Chester spends a lot of time describing the beauty he sees around him. Think about some aspect of nature that you think is beautiful and describe it so that someone else can see it through your eyes.

RESEARCH QUESTIONS

1. What causes depression? What are the symptoms and how is it treated?

2. How are adobe houses made?

3. Research the meaning of dreams.

4. What causes homesickness?

5. How can children help an alcoholic parent?

6. Chester says the stars are more brilliant in Santa Fe than in Clifton. What is the scientific explanation?

7. Research the history of Fiesta de Santa Fe and the origins of the burning of Zozobra.

PRAIRIE SONGS
Pam Conrad

SUBJECTS: *pioneers, prairie life.*
SUMMARY: *Louisa's family lives on the prairie and sees all the good things about prairie life. When a doctor and his wife come from the East to live on the prairie, the wife sees only the isolation of the prairie and the hardship. She eventually goes crazy and dies.*
COMMENTS: *Compare/contrast skills are easily taught through this book.* Prairie Songs *can be read in conjunction with history classes about the pioneers.*

VOCABULARY

soddy
prairie
ice house
pioneers
delicate
streetcar
horizon
muslin
vastness
portraits

DISCUSSION QUESTIONS AND WRITING EXERCISES

1. Why does Louisa think people from back East are not very strong?

2. Why does Mrs. Whitfield consider books, lace curtains, and poetry to be frivolous?

*3. Compare and contrast Mrs. Berryman to Louisa's mother.

*4. Describe in your diary your first impression of Mrs. Berryman.

5. Pretend you are Mrs. Berryman. Write a letter to send back East describing your thoughts about living in a sod house.

6. Why did the Indian man and woman run away when they saw the picture of Jesus on the cross?

7. Mrs. Berryman seems to have a hard time adjusting to her surroundings. Do you think it was appropriate for Louisa's mother to start off talking about Indians during their picnic? Why?

*8. Compare and contrast how Louisa and her mother see the prairie with how Mrs. Berryman sees it.

9. Do you think Mrs. Berryman should learn to shoot? Why?

10. Why was it hard for Louisa's mom to ask Mrs. Berryman to teach her children?

11. Is it good to own and carry a gun if you don't know how to use it? Explain.

12. How can the lonely prairie be a comfort to Louisa?

13. Have you ever been lonely and enjoyed it? Explain.

14. Mrs. Berryman reads Louisa one of Tennyson's poems about wanting to die. Do you think Mrs. Berryman wants to die? Explain.

15. Louisa is comforted by the lonely prairie, a blank wall, and a stretch of clean, flawless sand down at the river. What comforts you when you see it? Why?

16. Mrs. Berryman believes the broken crib is a sign that she and the baby will be destroyed. Do you believe in signs? Why?

17. Mrs. Berryman said she won't put her baby in a drawer like a savage. Does she really believe Louisa and her family are savages? Explain.

18. Do you think Paulie really wanted to kill his mother? Why?

19. Why does Louisa think Mrs. Berryman is dead?

20. How come Mrs. Berryman and Louisa's mother don't help bury the baby and there are no words spoken over him?

*21. Write out what you would say if you were to speak at the baby's funeral.

22. Why is Doc Berryman surprised that his soddy leaks?

23. Why does Mrs. Berryman say her books are dying?

24. When the cattle are all huddled together to stay warm in the snow, Louisa's mother comments that the cattle are smarter than the people. What is she really trying to say?

25. Who burned Mrs. Berryman's books—she or Doc, and why?

*26. Pretend you are Lester 40 years from now. Tell your grandchildren about your encounter with the two Lakota Indians.

RESEARCH QUESTIONS

1. How did the Lakota tribe treat settlers in Nebraska?

2. How did the Lakota tribe live?

3. What was a day in the life of a prairie woman like?

4. How many cases are there of people going mad in pioneering times?

5. What causes people to go mad?

6. What percentage of babies died in pioneering times?

7. What conditions caused more babies to die back then?

RANDALL'S WALL
Carol Fenner

SUBJECTS: *being poor, social outcasts.*
SUMMARY: *No one likes Randall because he smells. His social worker doesn't care about him nor his family. Randall spends all of his time at school drawing. One of his classmates, Jean, befriends him and helps him clean up. Once his teacher sees his drawings and decides he is gifted, she begins to help him and gets other people involved. Eventually Randall goes to live with his uncle.*
COMMENTS: *This is a book that definitely needs to be read. Students need to see that all people have feelings and need friends and help. People need to see people for what they are on the inside and not judge them on appearance.*

DISCUSSION QUESTIONS AND WRITING EXERCISES

1. Everyone says Randall smells and so they stay away from him. What would you do if a classmate smelled?

2. A classmate states that water is free. Is this true?

3. If you knew someone has had lice, what would you think about that person? Why?

4. What is the wall that Randall's sisters tell him about?

5. Why does Miss Grable object to the pictures Randall drew of his mother? Do you agree that Randall's pictures are inappropriate? Why?

6. The principal uses the right to privacy as an excuse not to help Randall. Does the right to privacy come before a person's well-being? Explain.

7. What impact does Randall's teacher's words about his bug bites and filth have on Randall?

*8. Write about a time when something a teacher said to you or about you affected you deeply.

9. Do you believe the social worker tried hard enough or cared when she went to Randall's house and left without seeing if anyone was home? Why?

10. Why do you think Randall was fascinated by Jean's black eye?

11. Who showed the most concern for Randall: Jean, his teacher, or the social worker? Why?

12. Randall doesn't have a clue as to why the other kids avoid him. Why?

13. Jean's father always says we are to be responsible for our fellow man. In what way? How are we to be responsible for Randall?

*14. Pretend you are Randall. Write in your school journal what it was like having Jean speak to you.

15. Why is Randall so surprised that Jean can eat so slowly?

*16. Write from the point of view of the bath tub about having Randall bathe.

17. Why do you think Jean's mother was comforted when she thought Randall was rich? Is she prejudiced? Explain.

18. Was it right for Randall's teacher to go through his desk and look in his notebook? Why?

19. Why did Randall pass out?

20. Why does Randall shake when he realizes his wall is not there while he waits for school to start?

21. Did everyone want to help Randall because he was talented or because he needed help?

22. What types of things cause walls to be built?

23. Tom Lord is too proud to put his family on welfare. Would you accept welfare or let your family starve? Why?

*24. You are Randall's teacher. Write a letter to the Lions Club requesting aid for Randall and his family. Explain what is needed and why.

RESEARCH QUESTIONS

1. What is the right to privacy and what does it cover? Are there exceptions?

2. What can the public health department do for families like Randall's?

3. What agencies give aid to impoverished families?

4. How many families in your town are aided by the public health department or social services?

5. What is the process one must go through to get aid?

6. How many families today live without water or electricity?

THE REVOLVING DOOR STOPS HERE
Phyllis Anderson Wood

SUBJECTS: *foster children, belonging.*
SUMMARY: *Eric has been moved about from family to family in the foster care program. Each foster parent eventually has to give up Eric due to the wife's drinking or to running out of space. Eric feels he doesn't belong anywhere. His high school counselor takes him in and when they move they invite Eric to go with them. After Eric graduates they tell him he can stay, that he is a permanent part of their family.*
COMMENTS: *I highly recommend this book. Many people have the impression that all foster kids are bad. This book shows it is untrue. Through this book students will learn to appreciate what they have.*

VOCABULARY

foster
juvenile hall
placement
social worker
alcohol treatment center
asthma
wheezing
guardian
agency
disqualified
licensed
group home
case history

DISCUSSION QUESTIONS AND WRITING EXERCISES

1. What is your idea of the perfect home and parents?

2. How bad would your home have to get to cause you to want to live somewhere else? Explain.

3. Eric's mother was killed by a drunk driver. Knowing this, why do you think Eric wants to stay with Olive when she has a drinking problem and has driven drunk?

4. Why do you think Eric wants to cover for Olive with the police officer when she has a wreck while under the influence of alcohol? If you were Eric, would you tell? Explain.

5. What do you think would be the best way to help Olive?

6. Eric makes the statement, "Living with Joe matters to me a lot more than Olive's drinking does." Why does he feel this way?

*7. Write a paper explaining the advantages and disadvantages of taking a seventeen-year-old into your home instead of taking a small child.

8. What are some of the problems foster children must cope with?

*9. Imagine you have never seen your father and you have the opportunity to write him a letter. Think about what you would tell him and write a sample letter.

10. Why does counting help Eric breathe better faster?

11. What are some of the consequences of being laid off indefinitely?

*12. Pretend you are Eric. Write in your journal how you feel about being told you have to leave Faye Smuin's home.

13. What does Lorna mean when she tells Eric to view the Davidsons as friends instead of as family?

14. What do the Davidsons teach Eric about friendships?

15. Why would Eric think he is not wanted because Susan is having a baby?

*16. Write a letter to be given to the baby when he is older, telling about the first time you saw and held him.

17. How does Roger show he trusts Eric? Be specific.

18. What does Eric mean by his statement that his dream had turned into a nightmare?

19. Why does Eric's father give Eric the stock and check?

20. Why does Eric not accept the money and stock? Do you think he made the right decision? Explain.

21. Roger tells Eric's class that everyone needs a dream. What becomes Eric's new dream in Fern Creek?

*22. Write about the dream you have for yourself.

23. Waldo thinks Eric knows a lot about girls because he is a city boy. What would make Waldo think this?

24. What are other stereotypes that people hold about city people?

RESEARCH QUESTIONS

1. Who can be a foster parent and what kind of training is involved?

2. What do social workers do and what kind of training is involved?

3. How many foster kids are in your city, state, country?

4. What kind of kids become foster kids and what is the procedure for being placed in a foster home?

5. What is the average stay in a foster home and how many homes on average does a foster child stay in?

6. How many years do most children stay in foster care?

7. What does it cost the state to keep one child in foster care for one year?

RUMBLE FISH
S.E. Hinton

SUBJECTS: *gangs, belonging.*
SUMMARY: *Rusty-James admires his brother, Motorcycle Boy. He wants to be just like him. They enjoy gang fights and being cool. Rusty-James usually has to steal food to eat because his father drinks up all the money. Rusty wants to belong to anything but Motorcycle Boy says belonging is not for him. Eventually Motorcycle Boy gets killed and Rusty-James is on his own.*
COMMENTS: *I like* Rumble Fish *because it shows that people in gangs are going nowhere and are just throwing their lives away. It is a good book to read to get students to wake up and smell the roses.*

VOCABULARY

rumble
switchblade
hood
junkies
D.T.s
jimmied

DISCUSSION QUESTIONS AND WRITING EXERCISES

1. Biff says he is going to kill Rusty-James. Why?

2. Rusty-James likes the zoo. He says the animals remind him of people. If someone said an animal reminded them of you, what animal would it be and why?

3. Rusty-James loves to fight. It makes him feel high; as if he could do anything. Why do people like to fight? Can Rusty do anything or is this an illusion? Explain.

4. Smokey says being in a gang is out of style now. Is being in a gang in style today? Explain.

5. If someone wanted to fight you, would you show up? Would you consider yourself a coward if you didn't? Why?

6. What are the rules for gang fights? Why do they have rules?

7. Rusty-James won't go to the hospital after being knifed. Why?

8. Motorcycle Boy was expelled from school for having perfect semester tests. How can this be done if he hasn't cheated?

9. Rusty-James thinks Motorcycle Boy is the coolest person in the whole world. Why?

*10. Write a paper titled "The Coolest Person."

11. Rusty-James is in all the classes for dummies. Is it good to separate kids and put all the smart kids together? Explain.

12. What would you do if a teacher offered you five bucks to beat up a mouthy kid? Why?

13. Rusty-James doesn't have any money for food, etc., so he steals. What alternatives are open to him for getting what he needs?

14. Rusty-James's dad was a lawyer who is now a drunk on welfare. Speculate on how he got that way.

15. Rusty is knifed and his father says, ''Be more careful.'' What kind of attitude is this?

*16. Write out what your mother or father would say and do if you came home with a knife wound.

17. Motorcycle Boy doesn't have any friends, just admirers and enemies. Would you rather be admired or have a friend? Explain.

18. Motorcycle Boy doesn't drink because he likes control. Explain what drinking has to do with control.

19. Motorcycle Boy said he stopped being a little kid when he was five years old. How can this be?

20. Why did Motorcycle Boy go to find and see the mother who abandoned him?

*21. Write out what you would say to your mother when you saw her after not hearing from her for years.

22. Why didn't Motorcycle Boy tell Rusty-James at first about seeing their mother?

23. When discussing gangs, Motorcycle Boy says, ''Apparently it is essential to some people to belong—anywhere.'' Is this true? What types of things do people belong to today and why?

24. Rusty-James is worried because Motorcycle Boy didn't belong—anywhere—he didn't want to. Why does this bother Rusty-James?

25. BJ says people follow leaders who are smart instead of tough, so Rusty-James could never lead a gang.

26. Rusty-James's dad says you can be different from the usual person but still be normal. What do you consider normal?

27. Why does Motorcycle Boy set the animals free in the pet store?

*28. Write a paper comparing and contrasting Steve's attitude toward life with that of Rusty-James.

*29. Everyone admires Motorcycle Boy. Write about who you admire the most.

RESEARCH QUESTIONS

1. What percentage of kids who drink a lot have a parent who is an alcoholic?

2. Is alcoholism inherited and if not, what causes it?

3. How many gangs are in your town?

4. Why do people join gangs?

5. What are the effects of alcohol on a person?

6. How many children are abandoned each year in your town? The United States?

7. What causes color blindness?

8. What percentage of males are color-blind? Of females?

SCARED STIFF
Willo Davis Roberts

> **SUBJECTS:** *kidnapping, fraud.*
> **SUMMARY:** *Rick's mother is kidnapped by the owners of the trucking company where she works when she discovers they are defrauding insurance companies. She has hidden evidence that they are after. Rick and his brother stay with their uncle in a trailer park while their mother is missing and sneak into an abandoned amusement park. Rick and his new friends in the park follow leads to find his mother and lead the criminals on a trip through the amusement park.*
> **COMMENTS:** *From the reading, students will learn how an amusement park is operated. Scared Stiff lends itself easily to a study of problem-solving skills.*

VOCABULARY

dispatcher
abandon
gondolas
ransom
canals
tortured
suspect
evidence
investigate
electric eyes
hostage
retrace
trespassing
trigger
ransacked

DISCUSSION QUESTIONS AND WRITING EXERCISES

1. Is it true that trouble comes in threes? Can you give examples?

2. When Rick's mom asks her husband if he was in on the robbery, what does that tell you about her?

3. Rick asks how a person can stop loving someone. How can one?

4. If your parents disappeared, who would you call and why?

*5. Write out a missing person's poster for your mom who has disappeared.

6. Connie stays in the park when his father is drunk. Why doesn't he turn his father in? Would you? Explain.

*7. Make a list of questions you would ask if you were interviewing all the neighbors in a missing person investigation.

8. If you were going to hide something valuable in your home where would you put it so that someone ransacking your home wouldn't find it?

9. Why is it okay to break into the park but not into the rides? Is there a difference? Explain.

10. How do the men in the black sedan know to come to the trailer park?

11. One of the men offers Connie and Julie five dollars to find Rick and Kenny. The other man says, "Money gets to everybody if you offer enough." Is this true?

12. Are there things you would not do for money? Explain.

13. Where would you hide in an amusement park?

14. Did the owners of the park do a good job of locking the park and securing it before abandoning it? Name all the ways the owners messed up.

15. Being surrounded by the police, Packard still refused to release Kenny and come out. Why?

*16. Imagine you are a reporter. Write up the story of the kidnapping and capture for the paper.

17. Describe your favorite amusement park ride.

18. Would you commit a crime or do something wrong if someone were threatening to harm your family if you didn't? Are there circumstances in which you would not? Explain.

RESEARCH QUESTIONS

1. It takes two keys to operate amusement park rides. What other safety devices do amusement parks have?

2. What procedure does the police follow in a missing person report?

3. What are the options for a child who has been abandoned?

4. How many children are abandoned by their parents?

5. How do you preserve a footprint that is made of water?

6. Where do low-income or retired people go when they lose their homes? Who helps them?

7. How much money do insurance companies lose a year due to fraud?

8. What is the penalty for kidnapping? Hijacking?

THE SCARIEST NIGHT
Betty Ren Wright

SUBJECTS: *foster children, prodigy, elderly, family relationships, death.*
SUMMARY: *Erin and her parents spend the summer in a run-down apartment building so their new foster child, Cowper, can take piano lessons. He is a gifted musician and Erin feels left out and ignored. She spends her time with the elderly people in the building and learns through them to make her own magic.*
COMMENTS: *Students will learn what it is like to be old and alone. Erin has a hard time accepting a new person into her family. Learning to accept people and situations and learning to live up to your dreams and not your parents' dreams are important lessons taught.*

VOCABULARY

peculiar
resentment
medium
seance
conservatory
genius
foster
jealousy
railroad flat
incinerator chute
dungeon
incense
ventriloquist
audition

DISCUSSION QUESTIONS AND WRITING EXERCISES

*1. Write a want ad for the paper about your missing cat, Rufus.

2. Erin's mother says Cowper is a genius and that makes him different. Why?

3. How would you feel if you lost both your parents like Cowper did?

4. What does Molly mean when she says people can make their own magic?

5. Cowper states that you can't make a friend in one day. Friendship takes a long time. Explain why.

*6. Write in your diary your thoughts and feelings upon entering your summer apartment for the first time.

7. Do you think it was right to smuggle Rufus into the apartment knowing that the rules of the building do not allow pets? Justify your answer.

8. How would you feel if you took a class and found that you were to be the only child in a class full of adults? Would you take it anyway? Why?

9. Describe Erin's attitude about being in Milwaukee for the summer.

10. What do you think really happened when Erin thought the lion talked?

11. Why does Mr. Barnhart give Erin a lecture after she put out his kitchen fire?

12. Why does Molly Panca think her dolls are real?

13. Is Molly Panca crazy? Support your answer.

14. Molly hints around through Margaret Mary that Erin is jealous of Cowper and is choosing to be left out. What can Erin do not to be left out of her family's fun?

15. Why doesn't Cowper want to play the piano anymore?

16. Is it okay for parents to force small children with talent to be famous? Explain.

17. Why doesn't Erin think she's special to her parents?

*18. Write your own mystery story or play.

19. Why don't Erin's parents believe Cowper when he says he wants to stop playing for a while?

20. Why does Cowper believe Erin's parents will hate him if he stops playing the piano?

21. Cowper says Erin's parents don't want to know how he feels. Why not?

22. Why would Cowper risk his life by jumping onto a porch five stories high? Does Cowper know it is dangerous?

23. What does Cowper think about while he is on the ledge?

24. Erin wants to tell her parents about the ledge. When is it okay to tattle?

25. Does Molly Panca fake the seance? If she did, explain how.

26. Are you an evil person if you want to get rid of your little brother? Is it normal to have a thought like this? Explain.

27. How does telling someone you love them help them make good decisions?

28. What different things let Erin know she really loves Cowper?

29. Do you feel Erin's treatment by her parents all summer was fair? Explain.

*30. Write a speech to give at a memorial service telling what kind of person Molly Panca was.

31. Why was Erin given Margaret Mary and not one of the other dolls?

*32. Write an ending to the story telling what Erin and Cowper do for the rest of the summer.

33. What kind of adjustments must a person make when a child is adopted or a foster child is taken into a family?

34. What kind of problems does a foster child have to overcome?

SCORPIONS
Walter Dean Myers

SUBJECTS: *gangs, violence, guns.*
SUMMARY: *Jamal's brother, who was the leader of the Scorpions, is sent to prison. Jamal has to decide whether or not to step in and become the new leader of the gang. He is given a gun and gets into all kinds of trouble, eventually leading to the death of some of the members.*
COMMENTS: Scorpions *shows how bad gang life is and that being in a gang will get you nowhere. This book can help students see how hopeless gang life is.*

DISCUSSION QUESTIONS AND WRITING EXERCISES

1. When Jamal is tardy, why does Jamal's principal say he'd have Jamal's mother come to school but he figured she didn't care about his education either?

2. Why does the owner of the grocery store tell Jamal he is no welfare department when Jamal tries to buy groceries from him?

3. Why does Jamal get upset when Tito reveals that his cousin Randy is in jail?

4. Why doesn't Jamal want Randy to get out of jail? Would you?

5. Why does Dwayne pick on Jamal? What advice would you give to Jamal about how to deal with bullies?

6. Why would the Scorpions consider Jamal to be their new leader when he is so young?

7. Why does Jamal take the gun from Mack?

8. Would you want to be the leader of a gang? Why? What would make you afraid?

9. Should the Scorpions make Jamal their leader because he is good at it or because they fear the gun?

10. The Scorpions say killing runs in the blood when they see Jamal has a gun. Will Jamal use the gun just because Randy did? Why?

11. Why does Jamal want his dad back?

12. What causes men to turn to alcohol after losing a job?

*13. Pretend you are Jamal. Write a letter telling your dad how you feel about how he treats you on his visits.

14. Jamal wonders if Randy thought everything was going to be easy and then things got messed up. Do people who are criminals or who kill people plan on killing them, or does it just happen? Explain.

*15. Pretend you are Jamal and are thinking about leaving home because of the fight in the storeroom. Write a note to your mom explaining why you aren't going to be around anymore.

16. Jamal feels good about having a job. Have you ever had a part-time job? How did it make you feel and why?

17. Abuela kicks Tito out of the house when she finds the gun. What would happen at your house if your parents found a gun you had hidden?

*18. Jamal's mom tells Tito that his grandmother still loves him no matter what. Write about an example from your life where your parents got very angry but still loved you. Is there anything you can do that would make your parents stop loving you?

19. Why does Mr. Gonzalez fire Jamal? Would you have? Why?

20. When Jamal learns Randy was stabbed, he says they don't make things happen, things happen to them. Is this true? How can you make things happen for you and should you?

21. How would you dispose of a gun?

22. Jamal says everybody is scared of something. What are you scared of?

23. Jamal says the gun is just to scare people. Is it okay to have a gun if you are not willing to use it? Explain.

24. Why do Angel and Indian beat up Jamal after Jamal gave up the Scorpions?

25. Why did Tito shoot Angel and Indian?

26. Why does Mack tell everyone he shot Angel and Indian?

27. Why does Tito get sick at home after the shooting? What is wrong with him?

*28. Write about a time you were sick because of something you felt.

29. Why does Tito go to the police and tell the truth? Would you have? Why?

30. Why won't Abuela let Jamal see or talk to Tito?

31. Why does Tito say he doesn't want Jamal's picture of him because he doesn't look like that anymore? How is he different?

32. Jamal's mom makes him start going to church. Will this make a difference? Explain.

33. Why does Jamal live in fear? Do all kids live in fear? Explain.

*34. Compare and contrast Jamal and Tito.

35. Why wasn't the shooting in the park in the newspaper?

*36. Pretend you are a teacher or school counselor. Write up a report on Jamal.

*37. Do you believe Jamal is basically good or bad? Give specifics to back up your statement.

RESEARCH QUESTIONS

1. How many people get stabbed or killed in prison?

2. How many weapons are found in the schools in your city?

3. How many gangs are there in your town?

4. What are the ages of gang members?

5. How much does it cost to appeal a verdict?

6. What happens to people who try to leave a gang?

SHADOW BROTHERS
A.E. Cannon

SUBJECTS: *Indians, track, relationships, belonging.*
SUMMARY: *Henry's father takes him off the reservation and sends him to live with the family of his longtime friend. Marcus and Henry are best friends and run track together. Henry has a run-in with an Indian from a different tribe who has an attitude. Through running track and living with Marcus's family, Henry realizes he needs to be around his own people and learn who he is. Henry returns to the reservation.*
COMMENTS: *Through this multicultural book, students can learn the importance of their heritage. Students can research their own heritage.*

VOCABULARY

hearse
Navajo
Utes
Paiute
hataali
foster
reservation
medicine man
ya-tah-hey
homesick
Mormon
insincere
culture
hogan
traditions
rituals
Hopi

DISCUSSION QUESTIONS AND WRITING EXERCISES

1. What kind of picture or first impression comes to mind when you see a kid's car is a hearse?

*2. Write a paper called "The Me Nobody Knows."

3. Miss Brett tells Henry, "You have a real gift. That means you also have a responsibility to develop it." Why?

4. When Marcus is bored in class he makes lists. What do you do?

5. Can being homesick make you really sick? Explain.

*6. Describe a time when you were really homesick and what you did about it.

7. Henry thinks girls sometimes jump to false conclusions about beautiful girls because they feel threatened. Explain how they feel threatened and whether you agree or not.

8. Is it right to think two people should be friends based on their race or the color of their skin? Why?

9. What is meant by "Anglos are controlled by time, Navajos aren't"?

10. Diana rescues animals. She finds a cat tied in a bag in a dumpster and rescues it at midnight. What does the rescue tell you about Diana?

11. Frank tells Henry he doesn't want to fit in. Why not? What would make someone feel this way?

12. Marcus believes you can tell a lot about someone's personality by looking at the inside of their school locker. If we looked inside of yours, what would we learn about you?

13. Why do you think Henry hates Frank so much?

14. Diana's cause is saving animals because she really cares about them. What cause do you really care about and why?

15. Why do you think Henry is not willing to take Celia to the Spring Fling in the hearse?

16. Why does Diana think Celia is using Henry?

17. Why does Henry hit Marcus after he loses the race to Frank?

18. Why do you think Henry didn't realize he was angry at his father for sending him away?

19. Why do you think Celia made Henry look like a white boy in her painting?

20. Henry says he is nothing because he doesn't fit in either world. What does being nothing mean?

*21. Write a poem about loneliness, friendship, or nothingness.

*22. Write out a conversation between Frank and Marcus when they meet again five years from now.

RESEARCH QUESTIONS

1. What was on the land before your town was built?

2. Research the beginnings of your town.

3. Henry's school is named for an Indian chief. How did your school get its name?

4. How many animals are annually dumped and killed by owners or are known to be abandoned?

5. How many animal rescues are made each year?

6. What are the cultural differences between Navajos and Anglos?

7. What is life like on a Navajo reservation?

SKEETER
K. Smith

SUBJECTS: *prejudice, black history, hunting.*
SUMMARY: *Joey and Steve get lost in the woods and run into Skeeter, an old black man, who shows them the way home. Later the boys sneak back to Skeeter's place and secretly develop a strong friendship with him. He teaches the boys to hunt and gives them his guns. When Joey gets hurt in an accident, their relationship is brought out into the open. Steve learns to accept Skeeter as a man and loses his prejudice.*
COMMENTS: *This is an excellent piece of historical fiction showing how the black man was treated many years ago. It shows Skeeter as a man with feelings and forces students to face their own prejudices and fears.*

DISCUSSION QUESTIONS AND WRITING EXERCISES

1. Joey won't admit he is lost. Why not?

2. Joey believes it is okay to go into Skeeter's woods and follow him because he'd get a good story out of it. When is a good story worth doing something wrong? Give an example.

3. Why is it wrong to kill the rabbit and leave it?

4. How do you know Steve is prejudiced? Give examples.

5. After Skeeter's first encounter with Joey and Steve he says, ''Well, Lord, they's not what I expected, but they's finally come.'' What does he mean?

6. Skeeter got his name because he never lit long, like a mosquito. If you got a nickname according to how you acted, what would it be and why?

*7. Skeeter says you must never break promises you make to yourself and you must have goals. Write out some goals for yourself and make yourself a promise.

8. Why is it important to keep promises you make to yourself?

9. What is prejudice and why is it wrong?

*10. Pretend you are Abraham Lincoln. Write out what you will tell Joey's puppy about going hunting with Joey and Steve.

11. Why does Skeeter make Joey apologize to the rooster for getting the hens upset?

12. Why does Skeeter prefer to isolate himself from people?

13. Why is Steve bothered by the fact that he cares for Skeeter?

14. Do you agree with Skeeter's decision to allow Joey to hunt alone? Why?

*15. Pretend you are Skeeter. Write out an argument to convince Joey not to hunt alone.

16. What could you do to keep Joey from hunting alone?

17. What does Joey realize about himself as he is lying in the stream?

18. Why does Joey's dad suspect Joey and Skeeter have some sort of ongoing relationship when he comes with the rescue squad to get his son?

19. Skeeter says Joey doesn't respect anything. How does he know this?

*20. Skeeter gives Joey advice about how to get a woman. Pretend your best friend asked you this question. Write out how to get a woman or a man to like you.

21. When speaking of women, Skeeter says, "Don't go throwin' yo' pearls before no swine, no fox neither." What does he mean?

22. Skeeter says that what he'd change about his life everyone knows. It's written on the hanging tree. Explain what he means.

*23. Compare and contrast Steve and Joey.

24. How has Steve changed in his attitude toward Skeeter from his first meeting with Skeeter to the end?

25. Why is it harder to accept Jerry's death by drowning than Peter's death by shooting in the Korean war?

26. Why doesn't Skeeter call the boys by their real names?

27. Why was it okay for blacks like Skeeter to be proud as long as they didn't act that way?

28. Do you believe it is Steve's fault that Skeeter is dead? Explain.

29. Skeeter wants animals and birds by his grave. What would you want around yours?

30. Why can't Steve kill the old mule?

31. Who learned more from Skeeter—Steve or Joey, and why?

32. What is the one most important thing Skeeter taught the boys excluding hunting?

33. Why would Steve and Joey's parents allow them to take Skeeter on the hunting trip knowing Skeeter would probably die on it?

*34. Imagine you are Steve and Joey's friend. Write out how you can help them get over Skeeter's death.

RESEARCH QUESTIONS

1. The treatment of blacks in the early 20th century.

2. What is Bull Connor known for?

3. How did the civil rights movement begin?

4. How old do bucks get?

5. What is the largest recorded number of points on a rack and what do the points tell?

6. Before the civil rights movement, blacks were not allowed to swim in public pools. What else were they not allowed to do?

7. When were blacks first admitted to white hospitals?

8. What kind of jobs could blacks get in the early 20th century?

9. Find instances of blacks being rounded up and told how to vote.

THE SKELETON MAN
Jay Bennett

SUBJECTS: *gambling, murder mystery.*
SUMMARY: *Ray's uncle gives him a lot of money and then supposedly kills himself. Many people are after the money that Ray's uncle got from gambling. In trying to get the money, people turn up murdered and Ray's life is threatened. Ray learns who has been doing the murdering and makes an important decision concerning the money.*
COMMENTS: Skeleton Man *shows the evils of gambling. It is a good suspense novel. Students can keep guessing where the money came from and who the murderer is throughout the book.*

VOCABULARY

compulsive
gambler
slot machine
casino
eternal
cynical
despondently
boardwalk
deceiving
gullible
stakes
desolate
somber
silencer
melancholy

DISCUSSION QUESTIONS AND WRITING EXERCISES

1. Where do you think the $30,000 came from?

2. Why is Ray to tell no one about the money?

3. Why do you think Ed killed himself? Do you think anyone ever does everything they have ever wanted to do?

*4. Write out what you want to have done in your lifetime.

5. If you were Ray, would you tell your mother about the money since she doesn't understand why Edward didn't give him anything? Why?

6. What does Edward mean when he tells Ray's mother he is a skeleton man?

7. Laurie says everybody gambles. Why does she say this? Is it true?

8. Laurie says she gambles for fun. Why do you think people gamble?

9. Ray says gambling is like beating a dead horse. What does he mean?

10. If you were Ray, would you have loaned the man nine dollars for parking? Why?

11. Do you believe the nine dollars was for parking or for gambling? Why?

12. Should you ever loan money to a gambler? Why?

13. The voice of the man who gave Ray the medal says Ray will become a liar, thief, and murderer. How so?

14. Is gambling a disease, as Ray thinks?

15. When Ray first meets Dawson, before he learns what Dawson wants from him, he feels Dawson is deadly and Ray is chilled to the bone. What makes him feel this way?

16. What is there about people that can make you mistrust them when you don't even know them?

17. Alice tells Ray that his uncle paid for the money with his life. What does this tell you about Ed's relationship with Ray?

18. Would you die in order to send a loved one to college? Why?

19. Alice loved and hated Ed. How can you both love and hate the same person? Give an example.

20. Alice tells Ray that Ed didn't want Ray to be ashamed of him so he didn't go to see him. Would you rather have a loving relative you know and see who has done something wrong or have no one but a distant person you respect? Explain.

21. Do you think the money belongs to Ray or Dawson? Why?

22. Why do you think Alice wrote out the suicide note knowing Ed had been murdered?

23. In his dream, Ray tells his father all gamblers lie. Why does he say this?

24. Pete tells Ray that when people become savages. you have to take on jungle ways. It's the only way to survive. Explain the statement and give an example.

25. If you were Ray, would you give the money to Dawson or keep it? Why?

26. Ray asks Dawson, "How does a human being turn into an animal?" How do they?

*27. Imagine you are Ray. Write in your journal how you felt when Alice said she thought of herself as your aunt and that Ed talked about you all the time.

*28. Write a letter to the police stating what has happened in case you are found murdered.

29. Dawson tells Ray that we don't control our destiny. Do you agree? Explain.

30. A skeleton man is one who is dead and yet still lives. How is this so? Give an example.

*31. Write a paper telling the pros and cons of gambling.

RESEARCH QUESTIONS

1. How does one earn the congressional medal of honor?

2. Research the history of Gamblers Anonymous.

3. What are the support groups for gamblers and how do they work?

4. How many people in the United States are addicted to gambling?

5. What percentage of people win in casinos?

6. How many states have legalized gambling?

SONG OF THE BUFFALO BOY
Sherry Garland

SUBJECTS: *Vietnam, customs, relationships, war.*
SUMMARY: *Loi wants to marry Quy but she is not allowed to because she is Amerasian. Her family has arranged for her to marry a very cruel man. After faking her death, Loi runs away to Saigon where Quy is to join her. They get separated and Loi learns she can go to America with the Amerasian program. There is a surprise ending.*
COMMENTS: *This factual book is an excellent study of Vietnamese customs. Compare/contrast skills can easily be incorporated. The devastation and results of a war that has been over for many years are shown.*

VOCABULARY

Da Nang
tamarind tree
ao dai
Viet Cong
con-lai
threshing
chaff
sheaves
citronella
agape
omen
Mandarin
frivolous
citadel
insolent
bovines

DISCUSSION QUESTIONS AND WRITING EXERCISES

1. Who do you think is the American soldier that Loi remembers? Why did Loi treasure the photograph of this man?

2. Why was it important that no one knew Loi was con-lai, half-American and half Vietnamese?

3. Loi didn't mind when rats ran across her feet. How would you feel about that?

4. How do you think Loi felt when people called her con-lai? How would you feel?

5. Loi was discriminated against because she was half American and half Vietnamese. How are people around you discriminated against? Is this fair? Explain.

6. Why do the Vietnamese soldiers steal from their own people?

7. Quy says that a respectable woman would drown herself rather than be raped, and kill a baby who was a product of rape. Would you? Why?

8. Do you think that parents should choose who their children will marry? Explain.

9. Why doesn't Khai want to tell Loi's uncle he is interested in her when he knows how awful Officer Hiep is?

*10. If you were Loi would you want to marry Officer Hiep? Write a letter to Uncle Long giving your reasons for either wanting or not wanting to marry him.

11. Why would Loi's mom sleep with an American soldier if they were on opposite sides during the war?

12. Why does Loi's mom allow Huong to scratch her and blame her when she delivers a dead, deformed baby?

13. Why were Loi and her mother blamed for the death of Huong's baby?

14. What could have happened that would have made Huong kill herself rather than live knowing she had a deformed baby?

15. Why does Khai refuse to see Loi?

16. Why does Officer Hiep demand that Loi stand naked before him at the pool? What kind of man is he?

17. Why is Loi not good enough for Khai but okay for Officer Hiep to the matchmakers?

18. If you were being forced to marry someone you didn't like, what would you do to prevent this from happening?

*19. Compare and contrast our marriage customs with Loi's.

20. What happens to Vietnamese who disobey their parents? What happens when you show you have a mind of your own?

21. Why is Officer Hiep willing to marry a halfbreed?

22. Why doesn't Officer Hiep say anything when he eats the rotten food?

23. How can Uncle Long let Loi marry a man who fought on the opposite side during the war?

24. Why did the Party take everything away from their countrymen when the war was over?

25. Loi saves her Uncle Long by agreeing to marry Officer Hiep. Would you have? Why?

26. Loi's mom says she almost wishes she hadn't had Loi—that she is too troublesome. Is she really troublesome and whose fault is it if she is? Explain.

27. Why does Loi expect Khai and her mother to want to go to America with her?

28. What do you think Loi hoped to gain by going to America?

29. How do you know Loi doesn't know anything about America?

30. Why does Loi's mother think Loi would not recognize an American?

31. Why is Loi surprised that Richard Smith has hair on his face?

32. Do all halfbreeds want to come to America? Explain.

*33. Joe has a certain view of America and Americans. Write a letter to Joe and describe the America that you know and some of the people who live around you.

34. Do you think it is wrong for people to steal food if they are starving? Explain.

35. Why doesn't Loi jump off the bus and take the next bus with Khai? Do you think Loi is selfish? Why?

36. All of Saigon is filled with beggars. How do you keep from giving away everything you have and not feel guilty? Loi gives cigarettes to a blind cripple because she thinks an American took his legs.

37. Why does the taxi driver tell Loi he will be waiting to take her back to the bus station? Why does no one think she can get to America?

*38. Imagine you are Loi. Write about your first seeing Saigon.

*39. You are Loi's Uncle Long. Write out a funeral speech for Loi.

40. Why would Loi let a thief help her?

41. Since no one wants to be a halfbreed, why does Joe?

42. Why would Joe, knowing nothing about America, want to leave his homeland?

43. Why does the policeman take a handful of Loi's cigarettes? Does she have no recourse?

44. Why does Joe hate the moon festival?

45. Why does Joe make light of every situation?

46. Loi thinks swindling a man who wants to use a girl's body isn't the same as stealing from some poor old woman who needed the money. What's the difference?

47. How does everyone in Saigon know that Loi is from the country?

*48. You are alone in a large city and know no one. Write out how you will survive and get what you need.

49. Why does honor mean so much that people ruin others' lives and their own for the sake of being honorable?

50. Why does Joe think that all Americans are rich?

51. Loi stays behind with Khai and lets Joe go to America in her place. Would you have? Explain.

52. If Loi had not seen Khai's carvings first, do you think she would have gone to America?

53. Loi says there is no honor in times of war. Explain.

54. If you left America forever, what would you miss and why?

55. If you were Loi and wanted to go to school, what would you have done?

56. Did the ending surprise you? How do you feel about what Loi's mother did to take care of her mother?

RESEARCH QUESTIONS

1. What happened in 1975 in Vietnam that caused Loi and her mother to leave Da Nang?

2. What are re-education camps? Why were they used after the war? Are they still used today?

3. Is the Amerasian Homecoming Program still operating?

4. What is the average height of a Vietnamese adult? What is the average height of an American adult?

5. How are babies who are half American and half Vietnamese treated today and why?

6. What caused the Vietnam war?

7. How do the Vietnamese live? What is their culture?

8. Explain the matchmaking custom and how it works.

9. Explain the process of growing rice from first planting to the market.

10. How many babies were deformed due to Agent Orange?

11. How does the result of the Vietnam war still affect the people today?

12. What is the Moon Festival, where did it originate, and how is it celebrated?

THE SPANISH KIDNAPPING DISASTER
Mary Downing Hahn

SUBJECTS: *kidnapping, adventure.*
SUMMARY: *While Felix and her family are in Spain on vacation, Felix meets Grace and lies to her about how rich her family is. Grace kidnaps Felix and her brother and sister and holds them for ransom. Grace wants the money to help save the hungry children of the world.*
COMMENTS: *This story shows how the rest of the world views Americans. To them we are all rich. It also shows that lying has consequences.*

DISCUSSION QUESTIONS AND WRITING EXERCISES

1. What would you do if you got separated from your parents in a foreign country?

2. Why does Felix lie to Grace about how rich her family is?

3. Grace says she is a citizen of the world from everywhere and nowhere. How can this be?

4. Phillip tells Amy and Felix to say they're sorry whether they mean it or not because their parents want them to. Does it make any difference if you don't mean it?

5. Who is to blame for being kidnapped: Felix, Amy, or their parents? Why?

6. Charles says that since they can't save all the starving children with $300,000, to save none. Is it worth it to do what you can if you can only save a few? Explain.

7. Is it okay to kidnap someone if it is for a good cause? Explain.

*8. Write out what you can do to help the poor and hungry and send it to the newspapers to ask for support.

*9. Write to a local agency asking how you can help the poor.

10. Do you think Grace is good or bad? Support your answer with facts.

11. If you were the children, would you have lied to keep Grace from going to jail? Why?

*12. Imagine you are a reporter. Write out your interview with one of the bus passengers about the hijacking and subsequent crash and capture of Charles and Orlando.

13. How do you think the lives of Felix, Amy, and Phillip will be affected as a result of their experience?

14. Should a person be required to know a few basic phrases of the language before visiting a foreign country? Explain.

15. Do you think the children will ever tell their parents what really happened? Why?

RESEARCH QUESTIONS

1. Grace says America's poor are richer than most of the people in her country. In what countries do the people live below poverty level?

2. What is being done to save the starving children of the world?

3. What organizations help feed children?

4. Compare the economics and standard of living of any Third World country with those of America.

5. What is the penalty for kidnapping in Spain?

6. What does an American citizen do if his/her passport gets lost?

7. What is the purpose of the American Embassy?

SUMMER OF THE MONKEYS
Wilson Rawls

SUBJECTS: *monkeys, rural life.*
SUMMARY: *Jay Berry finds several circus monkeys that have escaped from a train wreck. He wants the reward for returning them and goes about trying to catch them. Many funny incidents occur as time after time the monkeys outwit him.*
COMMENTS: *Excellent book for teaching problem-solving skills. The story is humorous and entertaining.*

DISCUSSION QUESTIONS AND WRITING EXERCISES

1. Why is it so important for Jay's parents to own land?

2. Why do animals respond to Daisy and not to Jay?

3. Who is the Old Man of the Mountains?

4. Jay believes in things bringing bad luck. What do you believe brings bad luck?

5. How did the big monkey know how to trip the traps?

6. Why was the big monkey laughing at Jay?

7. How did the monkey get the steel traps up the tree?

8. Design your own trap for catching monkeys.

9. When Jay's mother agrees to let him go to the bottoms with the net and his father helps dig the hole, how can Jay think he is going to be in big trouble for being bit?

10. Daisy announces that Jay and Rowdy might have hydrophobia. She wants to chain them to a fence post. Why won't Jay's mother let her if that is standard procedure?

*11. Jay Berry asks what he should say to the monkey to make friends with him. Write out how you would go about making friends with a monkey and what you would say to one.

12. Why does Jimbo take Jay Berry's pants?

*13. Pretend you are Jay Berry. Write out a believable story about why you came home without your pants.

*14. Jay Berry tells his mom the truth about how he got drunk but she doesn't believe him. Tell about a time you told the truth and were not believed.

*15. Jay Berry doesn't tell Daisy he's afraid of the storm too because boys aren't supposed to let girls know they are afraid. Write about a time you were afraid but pretended you weren't.

16. Why does Jay Berry wish for Daisy's leg to be fixed instead of for his getting the pony and .22?

17. If you made a wish in the fairy ring what would you wish for and why?

18. Do you believe crippled children can see and hear things others can't? Explain.

19. Why doesn't Jay Berry want to wait for the mare's leg to heal when it's the horse he really wants? Would you wait to get what you wanted? Why?

20. Jay Berry gets almost home with the mare before changing his mind. What finally makes up his mind to give the money to Daisy?

21. If you were Jay Berry, would you have kept the pony or helped your sister? Why?

22. Where did Daisy and Grandpa get the money for the pony and .22 they gave to Jay Berry?

23. Daisy's one request of Jay Berry is that he run with her. If you found that you were no longer crippled, what would you choose to do first that you couldn't do before and why?

24. When Jay Berry is left to run the house for six weeks he says he can cook. Why does he think he can cook?

25. Why do Jay Berry and his papa stop talking and get grumpy when they are alone for six weeks?

*26. Pretend you are Jay Berry. Describe seeing a train for the first time.

27. Jay Berry has never seen a black man before. Why not?

*28. Pretend you are Daisy. Describe what it is like to run for the first time.

*29. Pretend you are Jimbo. What is going through your mind when you see Jay Berry, Grandpa, and all those coconuts?

RESEARCH QUESTIONS

1. Where is the Cherokee Nation that Jay Berry lived on?

2. What are sharecroppers?

3. What causes children to be born crippled?

4. How expensive is an operation today to straighten a leg?

5. Chimpanzees—habitat, eating habits, etc.

6. What have chimps been trained to do?

7. How are monkeys caught in the wild?

8. How long does it take to train a chimp to do one trick?

9. How do trainers teach monkeys?

10. How much does it cost to train a monkey?

11. How much does it cost to buy a trained monkey?

12. Besides tricks, what tasks have monkeys been trained to do?

13. What is hydrophobia and what are the symptoms?

14. How do you choose a good horse?

SUSANNA SIEGELBAUM GIVES UP GUYS
June Foley

SUBJECTS: *dating, friendships, relationships.*
SUMMARY: *Susanna decides to give up guys. When her parents don't understand her not having a boyfriend she gets Ben to pretend to be her boyfriend. Susanna and Ben become good friends and he eventually really does become her boyfriend.*
COMMENTS: *This is not fluff but a very insightful book on teenage relationships. Ben learns Susanna's father can be a man and still like to bake bread. A discussion of role models can be helpful here.*

DISCUSSION QUESTIONS AND WRITING EXERCISES

1. Susanna chooses who she will ask to the Latin club banquet by how well they would look in a toga. What does this tell you about Susanna?

2. Susanna rates guys by their physical attributes. Have you ever done this? Why would you want to?

3. Susanna says going out with lots of boys is like going out with no boys at all. Explain.

4. Susanna tells Cassidy to tell Robby, ''I like you a lot, but we're spending too much time together. I really hope you'll understand.'' She says it's okay to hurt somebody's feelings, but when Cassidy says it to her, Susanna is hurt and offended. Does she have a right to be? Is it okay to say something to someone else you wouldn't want said to you? Why?

5. Susanna goes out with the girls and feels lonelier than when she was by herself. How can this be?

6. Susanna describes Ben as constantly moving, playing sports, showing no emotion, and goofy. Yet she is willing to play sports with him so he'll pretend to be her boyfriend. Is it worth it? Would you take anybody or tell your parents the truth? Why?

7. Susanna thinks Ben's book report is terrific. If Ben is smarter than he seems, why would he pretend to be a dumb jock?

8. Why is Ben shocked that Jerry likes to cook?

9. Ben's and Susanna's families make up words. What words have you or your family made up?

10. Susanna asks why Ben goofs all the time and she is surprised when he asks her why she does. How is Susanna a goof?

11. How does Ben know Susanna is jealous of Cassidy?

12. Why do you think Ben lied about his father being a business man, being good at sports, and his seeing him every weekend?

13. When Ben and Susanna are working on the *Roman Times,* Ben tells Susanna everything has got to be her way. She has to be the center of attention, know all the answers, and make up all the rules. Why does he say this? Give details from the story to back up his statement.

14. Is it possible to have a best friend and a boyfriend at the same time? Explain.

15. Cassidy wants to break up with Robby but he breaks up with her before she has a chance to tell him. She is upset. Why? Didn't she get what she wanted?

16. Susanna's favorite book is *Wuthering Heights*. What is yours and why?

17. Ben's mother used Ben as a character for her books. If your mom wrote a children's story with the character based on you, what would the character be and do and why?

*18. Pretend you are a reporter. Write an article about the story hour at the library.

19. Explain the statement, "I had to give up guys to find a boyfriend who was also a friend."

20. How has Susanna changed since the beginning of the book.

*21. Compare and contrast how Ben changed from the beginning of the book to the end.

RESEARCH QUESTIONS

1. Research the following names: Ty Cobb, Babe Ruth, Lou Gehrig, Mickey Mantle, Casey Stengel.

TAKING SIDES
Gary Soto

SUBJECTS: *moving, belonging, loyalties, prejudice.*
SUMMARY: *Lincoln and his mother move out of the slums into a nice neighborhood. Lincoln joins his new school's basketball team but has a hard time with team loyalty when they play his old team. He must also deal with his coach being prejudiced.*
COMMENTS: *In our transient society with so many students going from school to school, students need help in finding stability and a connection. This book talks about learning to adjust and fitting in.*

DISCUSSION QUESTIONS AND WRITING EXERCISES

1. Why does Lincoln like his new neighborhood at first and then change his mind? What's wrong with it?

2. Why is Lincoln offended by James's statement that Monica must be "full Mexican" because she knows Spanish so well?

3. When Tony accuses Lincoln of changing while on their way to the thrift shop, Lincoln says things change, people stay the same. Is this true? Explain.

4. Lincoln believes he is a traitor to Franklin by playing against them in basketball. Is he? Why?

5. Why doesn't Lincoln care about getting his TV back or at least finding out who stole it?

6. Why does Lincoln not eat his mother's food? She knows kids don't have jobs nor buy their own food.

7. Lincoln plans what to say when he shoots hoops with Monica, then chooses to go with whatever comes out of his mouth. When you know you are going to meet for a date, do you plan out the conversation? Why? What do you say?

8. Why didn't anyone call the police for a break-in in Lincoln's old neighborhood?

9. Why is Lincoln rude to Monica the day of the break-in?

10. Why would Lincoln say in front of his new team that they would lose?

11. Why doesn't Lincoln say, "We are going to lose" instead of "you are going to lose"? Isn't he part of the team?

12. Why does Lincoln feel he doesn't belong at Columbus?

*13. Pretend you are "Dear Abby." What advice would you give to Lincoln about dealing with prejudice?

14. Why did Coach Yesutis not want Lincoln to play even though he was one of the best players?

15. Columbus lost the game because the coach was prejudiced. When is the price you pay for being prejudiced worth it?

16. What makes people prejudiced?

17. Would you feel more at home at Columbus or at Franklin? Why?

18. When Lincoln played in the game he said he was going to play for himself and not for the pride of Columbus. He would not play to win. What does this tell you about Lincoln?

*19. Write an epilogue that takes place one year later.

RESEARCH QUESTIONS

1. Are there more break-ins in rich, average, or poor neighborhoods?

2. How have Mexicans been treated throughout the 20th century in America?

3. How have attitudes toward Mexican-Americans changed over the last twenty years?

THERE'S A GIRL IN MY HAMMERLOCK
Jerry Spinelli

SUBJECTS: *wrestling, girls in boys' sports.*
SUMMARY: *Maisie goes out for the wrestling team against the wishes of her parents, the coach, and team members. She sticks with it and overcomes the name-calling and attitudes of the school and community, earning the respect of her coach and team members.*
COMMENTS: *This is a hot issue for getting a debate going in class. Students love to take sides and discuss women in men's sports. Students will cover a large variety of skills in order to get facts to support their answers.*

VOCABULARY

stagnate
hormones
pin
rookies
monkey rolls
diamond-ups
stance
bout
crouch
shuffle
double arm tie-up
referee's position
escapes
sit-out
stand-up
take down
crotch ride
half-nelson

DISCUSSION QUESTIONS AND WRITING EXERCISES

1. Maisie feels her life is over because she didn't make cheerleader. Have you ever felt as if your life would be over if you didn't get a certain thing or have something happen your way? Explain.

2. Ever since Eric Delong spoke to Maisie at the pool, he's all she can think about. Tell about a time when all you could think about was a guy or girl instead of your work.

*3. Maisie says every now and then you need something like hormones to scare you into realizing how good you have it. What's good about your life?

4. If you are/were a girl, would you go out for a boys' sport? Why?

5. Should Maisie have told her parents up front that she went out for wrestling? Why?

6. Is Holly being a good friend when she confronts Maisie about going out for wrestling? Explain.

7. Would you make fun of a girl because she was on a boys' team? Why?

8. Is it right for Maisie's father not to let her quit the team just because some man demands that she quit? Why?

9. Why is George willing to be Maisie's friend?

10. What would you think about a girl who went out for boys' sports?

11. The coach says Maisie has moxie. What is moxie and why is it good to have?

12. Holly tells Maisie boys don't like girls who beat them in sports. Is this true? Explain.

13. Should a girl deliberately let a guy win in order to get a date? Why?

14. Maisie comes home from the pet store with a rat. If you did, would you be allowed to keep it? Maisie took the rat to save it from being eaten. What does this tell you about Maisie?

15. Would you rather practice wrestling holds on a girl/boy or a CPR dummy? Why?

16. Since everyone was faking when they practiced with Maisie, why did they wrestle her for real during the nutcracker?

17. Why does the team cheer Maisie when the nutcracker is over?

*18. Pretend you are Maisie. Write in your diary how you felt after the nutcracker was over.

19. Is winning by forfeit good? Why?

20. If you were a guy, would you wrestle a girl or forfeit knowing it could cause your team to lose? Why?

*21. Write a ''letter to the editor'' expressing your views on Maisie Potter's wrestling on the boys' team.

22. No one danced with Maisie at the school dance. Why?

23. Do you think she deserved the sign of runner-up for the hunkiest boy at the dance? Explain.

24. Maisie asks Eric Delong to dance but he dances with Liz instead. What does this tell you about Eric?

25. What kind of person is Liz Lampley?

26. Why were the Ravens' fans cheering for the rival team when Maisie lost?

*27. Pretend you are Maisie. What would you do if PK showed up and tackled your opponent for you? What would you say to her afterward?

28. According to the PTA, Maisie is corrupting the student body. In what way?

29. When the fans finally support Maisie at the last match is it because they like her or because she saved Tank's life?

*30. What has Maisie learned about herself through wrestling that has changed her? How is she a better person now for having wrestled?

RESEARCH QUESTIONS

1. What instances are there of women playing in male-dominated sports in the pros?

2. Is it allowed in your school or district for a woman to wrestle on a men's team?

3. Can girls legally be kept off a boys' team?

4. Can boys legally play on a girls' team?

THIS PLACE HAS NO ATMOSPHERE
Paula Danziger

SUBJECTS: *colonization, living on the Moon, friendships, moving.*
SUMMARY: *Aurora and her family go to the Moon to help colonize it. She doesn't want to go and has a hard time adjusting. She does make a friend and together they produce a play for the colonists. Through working together, Aurora learns a lot about herself and changes her attitude.*
COMMENTS: *This is an excellent book to read in conjunction with the science classes' study of the planets. Many Moon facts are covered in the material.*

VOCABULARY

telekinetic
cosmos
holograph
monolith
simulator
centrifugal
colonists
orbit
lunar
atmosphere
cloning
test tube babies

DISCUSSION QUESTIONS AND WRITING EXERCISES

*1. What are the pros and cons of having a robot for a school monitor?

2. Aurora and her friends are called the Turnips because they always turn up at places. What name would your group be called that reflects your group's character?

3. What would it be like to be a celebrity because you were conceived in space? How would your life be different?

4. This story takes place in 2057 and yet teenagers are still concerned with how they look and whether they will be accepted. Why can't these problems be solved?

*5. What are the pros and cons of having extrasensory perception? Would you want ESP?

6. What are the pros and cons of wearing mood clothes that change colors depending on what you are feeling or doing?

*7. Aurora takes a test to see what she knows about the Moon. Write a paper telling all you know about the Moon.

8. What does Neil Armstrong's statement, ''That's one small step for man, one giant leap for mankind'' mean?

9. What kinds of things do you think you'd need to learn to take a space flight or live on the Moon?

10. One family doesn't go to the Moon because they can't take their dog. Why can't they take it?

11. Why does April have no problem accepting Julie when Aurora does have a problem accepting her?

12. Why does it bother Aurora's parents to give up their large house on Earth but not bother them that they have cramped quarters on the Moon? What does being pioneers have to do with their attitude?

13. Every student has to do a service project and a community project. Aurora works with the small children for her service project. What service project would you pick out for yourself and why?

*14. Compare and contrast your town to Luna City.

*15. Write a poem about getting clean on the Moon.

16. There is no water on the Moon. Make a list of all the ways you use water in one week.

*17. The homes on the Moon have no televisions. Write to Aurora giving her suggestions on how to entertain herself.

18. Aurora's dad says she is not trying to like living on the Moon. What can Aurora do to try to adjust and fit in?

19. Why does Aurora feel she has to put on an act for the boys on Earth but not with Hal?

20. Aurora says Hal is a really different kind of friend. How?

*21. Write a play to be performed on the Earth showing what it's like to live on the Moon.

22. Aurora's family discusses what foods they miss the most. If you lived on the Moon, what Earth food would you miss the most?

*23. Aurora misses the weather on Earth. Write a descriptive paper telling about the different weather on Earth and how wonderful it is to someone who has always lived on the Moon.

*24. People will always live on the Moon if it is a way station for Mars. Write a paper to persuade the government to pay for beautifying Luna City.

25. Why does Aurora feel Mr. Wilcox has not been fair in giving the lead in the play to someone other than herself? Does she have a right to be angry? Why?

26. Mr. Wilcox tells Aurora that the universe does not revolve around her. Give examples to show how Aurora thinks it does.

27. Aurora and Juna once collected belly button lint and earwax because they wanted to have the most unusual collection in the world. If you collected something unusual, what would it be?

28. Aurora thinks the Turnips are cruel in their comments about the Moon kids. Isn't she the one who was cruel in her descriptions? Why have her feelings toward them changed?

29. Why does Aurora change her mind about going to live with her grandmother?

*30. Pretend you are Aurora. Write a letter to the Turnips telling them you are not coming back and why.

*31. Write an advertisement to get people to want to live on the Moon.

*32. Compare Aurora at the beginning of the trip to the Moon to how she is at the end of the play.

RESEARCH QUESTIONS

1. Research facts about the Moon.

2. Research the history of space travel.

3. Research the history of NASA and what they do.

4. Who is Neil Armstrong and what is he famous for?

5. What did Neil Armstrong and his group leave on the Moon and why?

6. What would you weigh on the Moon?

7. What kind of training must our astronauts have?

8. Who is Alan Shepard?

THE TROUBLE WITH LEMONS
Daniel Hayes

SUBJECTS: *murder, self-esteem.*
SUMMARY: *Tyler thinks of himself as a lemon. Everything is wrong. His parents are movie stars and he is left at home to be raised by the housekeeper. Tyler and Lymie find a dead body while swimming in the quarry. After reporting the find they go about solving the mystery. During the process Tyler discovers he is not a loser after all.*
COMMENTS: *The principal in this story prejudges Tyler because of who his parents are. Our self-worth comes from what people around us say to us. This book is excellent for discussing self-esteem and how our words can heal or hurt someone.*

VOCABULARY

quarry
asthma
adrenaline
trespassing
chlorinated
psychosomatic

DISCUSSION QUESTIONS AND WRITING EXERCISES

1. Why do you think Lymie spends his time ridiculing Tyler?

2. What kind of problems would you have if your parents or siblings were movie stars?

*3. Pretend you are Tyler. Write out a statement for the police about discovering the body.

4. Should older housekeepers and servants be called by their first names by children? Explain.

5. If you found a body while you were trespassing, what would you do? Why?

6. Why do you think people always flock to a disaster to gawk?

7. If you encountered a bully like Beaver at school and the coach was ignoring the situation, would you fight Beaver or take it? Why?

8. If you knew you were going to get beaten up on your way home from school, what would you do?

*9. Write in your journal how you felt after you fought Beaver in P.E.

*10. Tyler says that after he has humiliated himself, he feels better when someone else tells something embarrassing they have done. Tell about a time you did something really dumb.

11. After the pro wrestling match, Chuckie tells Tyler people like to feel that they are one of the good guys, and the easiest way to do that is to create bad guys and hate them and fight them. Is this true? Explain.

12. Tyler thinks that maybe he is a born loser, some kind of unfixable lemon doomed to screw up, no matter what. Is there such a thing as a born loser? Explain. How do people become losers?

13. Tyler believes deep down that he is the cause of his parents' divorce. What do you think? Can a kid cause a divorce? Explain.

14. Tyler's dad believes boys are supposed to keep things inside and work them out privately, and never in front of females. Do you agree? Explain. Is there a time to tell someone that you have a problem? When?

15. Mrs. Saunders tells Tyler that there are a million ways to be normal. Explain.

16. Should women be allowed to work and have children? Why?

17. How would you get someone to feel guilty enough to confess if you knew someone had done something wrong?

18. Chuckie says people control Tyler by getting him to react. What does this mean?

19. If you killed someone by accident, would you tell or try to cover it up? Why?

*20. Compare and contrast Mark's attitude with Jack's.

21. Tyler's mom says that life isn't just good guys fighting bad guys. Explain.

22. As a thirteen-year-old boy, is it okay to have your mom kiss you in public? Why?

*23. Pretend you are a reporter. Write up an article for the local paper on the circumstances of Boo Boo's death and the subsequent confession.

24. What do you think Mr. Blumberg means when he tells Tyler that he's sorry about everything?

RESEARCH QUESTIONS

1. What causes sleepwalking?

2. What causes recurring nightmares?

THE VOYAGE OF THE FROG
Gary Paulsen

SUBJECTS: *sailing, survival.*
SUMMARY: *David goes out on the sailboat he has inherited and is lost in a storm without proper provisions. He has many adventures as he learns to survive and eventually gets back home.*
COMMENTS: *Excellent book for teaching problem-solving skills and learning to think for oneself. Many animals and their behaviors are mentioned in the story. This is a good book to complement science studies about the ocean and the currents.*

VOCABULARY

bowsprit
pulpit
mast
boom
lifelines
portholes
hull
marina
harbor
breakwater
dock
lazaret
mainsail
spinnaker
winches
battens
tiller
beam
worm gear
cremated
cockpit
bow
stanchion
jib
luffing
helm
log
slip
boom
top hatch
hatch
reefing
halyard
forestay
knots

DISCUSSION QUESTIONS AND WRITING EXERCISES

1. Do you think a fourteen-year-old boy should be given the responsibility of scattering a relative's ashes all alone?

2. If you were cremated, what would you want done with your ashes?

3. Why do you think Owen chose David to scatter his ashes and why did he choose the ocean?

4. David wants to know everything about the Frog because Owen is a part of the Frog. If someone were to study an object in order to know you, what would that object be and why?

5. How is it that David can see Owen in the things of the Frog?

6. What things did David neglect to do at the beginning of the trip that he had been taught to do? Why do you think he neglected them?

*7. Write a journal entry about what you've seen and how you feel the first night out on the ocean.

8. What does the statement, "One hand for the sailor, one hand for the ship" mean? How would this saying help a frightened sailor?

9. What does David mean when he says, "Knowledge is everything, knowledge makes anything endurable," while the shark was attacking?

10. Why does David now have more understanding of the homeless and poor?

11. Why does David say the hunger and thirst is all in his mind when he hasn't eaten or drunk anything all day?

12. David changes his mind about throwing the trash overboard. He says that nothing is trash now. When he has nothing everything is valuable. Explain this statement.

13. Why do you think Owen didn't put emergency equipment on the Frog? Would you? Explain.

14. Why do you think David hates himself, his parents, everything? Have you ever hated like this? Explain.

15. David writes in the log, "I am alone." What does it mean to be truly alone?

16. Why does David consider himself and the Frog to be one?

*17. Pretend you are one of the whales. Write a narrative describing to other whales your experience of seeing David and the Frog.

18. After David's bad experience with the first storm, he chose to sail through the second one instead of remaining in the bay. If you were David, what would you have done and why?

19. When David encountered the whale research ship, he chose to sail home in the Frog instead of returning with them. Would you have left the Frog? Explain.

*20. Choose one of the experiences David had and write about it in the captain's log.

21. Do you believe David should call himself "Captain"? Why?

*22. Write a paper telling how David's view of the sea creatures changes from the beginning of his voyage to the end.

23. What do you believe is the most important thing David learned? Explain.

*24. Write a paper comparing David at the beginning of the voyage to how he is at the end of the voyage.

25. Do you think David survived because he was smart or because he was lucky? Give facts to back up your view.

*26. Rewrite the ending of the story with David not finding the research ship.

27. What do you believe to be the most important thing to take into account when sailing (wind, emergency equipment, knowledge, skill, etc.)? Why?

*28. Write a newspaper account of David's adventure.

29. If you could ask David one question about his trip, what would it be?

30. If you were to pack emergency equipment for a sailing vessel, what would you include and why?

31. Pretend you are David. Describe to the class one experience you had.

RESEARCH QUESTIONS

1. What is the behavior of whales? Of sharks?

2. Find instances of people surviving being lost at sea. How did they survive?

3. Draw and label the parts of a sailboat.

4. Map the trip David took.

5. What is the procedure for searching for missing boats? What percentage are found?

6. How far off course did David end up?

7. Have there been any instances of whales or sharks sinking boats or ships?

8. Today, how do vessels signal ships, planes, and people on land that they need help?

9. How does radar work? Why does the oil tanker not realize David is there?

THE WEIRDO
Theodore Taylor

SUBJECTS: *poachers, murder, disfigurement, bears, self-esteem, swamps.*
SUMMARY: *Samantha finds a dead body when she is little. A few years later, she is lost in the swamp and is rescued by Chip, who was disfigured in a plane crash. Chip is helping Telford track and count bears. When Telford turns up missing, Chip and Samantha search for clues and discover murder and poachers.*
COMMENTS: *This book is an excellent study of bears, habitats, and swamps. Samantha has to go against her father and stand up for what she believes in. This is a good book for discussing standing up for one's beliefs and for saving animals that are in danger.*

VOCABULARY

swamp
bog
marsh
poacher
bo'sun
boatswain
din
saw-toothed
weimaraner
bruin
defecate
craggy
hamlet
gamecocks
plantigrade
loblollies
rendezvous
triangulation
toiletry
aerial telemetry
mackinaw
dissertation
hypnotizing
surreal
blasé
caterwauling
peat moss
hibernate
refuge
Indian summer
bramble
taxidermy
moratorium

DISCUSSION QUESTIONS AND WRITING EXERCISES

1. How would you feel if you found a body in front of your house? Would your reaction be the same or different from Samantha's? In what ways?

2. When Officer Truesdale comes to investigate the murder, he begins by asking Sam where she goes to school and what grade she is in. Why does he do this?

*3. Write a letter to Samantha. Compare and contrast her home with the place where you live.

4. Would you pay $50,000 for a dog? Why?

5. Charles Clewt says there is a beauty in the swamp. How so?

6. Why would Sam go into the swamp alone after having been told her whole life not to, because it was dangerous?

7. Why would Sam choose to spend the night in the swamp when no one knew where she was?

8. Sam doesn't like the way she looks. Why?

9. If you could change your looks, what would you change and why?

10. How important is a person's appearance? Is it possible to like someone who is disfigured in some way? Do you think you could forget about Chip's appearance the way Sam did? Explain.

11. Chip bandages Sam's feet. She doesn't want him to. Why not?

12. Chip was burned in a plane crash. Do you think he looks in mirrors or turns away? Why?

13. Chip doesn't think any girl would date him because of his looks. Do you agree? Why?

14. Chip has been hiding from people because of his looks. Is this a good idea? Why? Imagine you are Chip's friend. Give him some advice about being around people again.

*15. Observe an animal (dog, cat, or other pet) during at least 30 minutes for at least five days. Keep a journal of what it does and eats, and how much it eats. Be as specific as possible.

*16. Chip wants to keep people from hunting on the reserve. Write a paper to persuade the Wildlife Service to continue the ban for another five years.

17. Chip tries to find out all he can about the black bears in the swamp. What kind of things should he learn about?

18. How can counting the bears help determine if the ban should be lifted or not?

19. If you were burned like Chip, what would you do when people rudely asked you about your face?

20. Sam believes Alvin Howell is sending her messages. Can you receive messages from the dead? Explain.

*21. Pretend you are Chip. Write in your journal about your first day working with Telford.

22. Why does Chip's father wish he had died in the plane crash with the rest of Chip's family?

23. Why does Chip's father feel guilty for being alive?

24. Telford says that nature provides checks and balances and that it is sometimes good to kill deer and bear. Why does Chip see all killing as wrong?

25. Do you think farmers should have the right to kill bears who are eating their crops? Explain.

26. When Sam meets Chip at Dunegan's, she thinks it would be easier to turn him down if he were whole. Why?

27. Is Sam going with Chip to look for Tom because she wants to or because she feels sorry for Chip?

28. Sam believes killing the bears is wrong. Would you go against your dad's beliefs about hunting if you disagreed? Why?

29. Have you ever been caught in the middle of a disagreement between two people you really liked/loved? How did you feel? How did you handle the situation?

*30. Write an article for *The Pilot* describing both sides of the bear-hunting issue. Present facts that represent both sides of the argument and not your opinion.

31. Is Chip being used by the environmental group to get sympathy?

*32. Sam doesn't understand why the poachers can't be caught. Write up a plan for catching the poachers.

33. Why is Sam intimidated by her father?

34. Why does Sam have Chip save Henry from the trap knowing how angry her father will be?

35. Is Chip brave or foolish to refuse to leave after the cabin window is shot out and the car tires slashed?

36. At the meeting, Sam's father asks if anyone else would like to speak, yet refuses to allow Sam to speak when she stands up. Why?

37. Why does Chip take off his cap and glove when speaking at the meeting?

*38. Write an ending to the story telling about what happens to Sam, her father, the poachers, and Chip.

RESEARCH QUESTIONS

1. What types of animals are native to the area in which you live?

2. What animals live in swamps?

3. What does it mean when a piece of land becomes a National Wildlife Refuge? How does a piece of land become a refuge?

4. What is the Fish and Wildlife Service? What is its purpose?

5. What is the purpose of organizations like Greenpeace and the National Wildlife Conservancy? Compare and contrast the methods these groups use to accomplish their goals.

6. What is hypnotism? Can it really help you remember things?

7. How many animals are killed yearly by poachers?

8. Research the habits and behavior of bears.

THE YEAR WITHOUT MICHAEL
Susan Beth Pfeffer

SUBJECTS: *missing children, family relationships.*
SUMMARY: *When Michael turns up missing on his way to a ball game, the community helps to search for him. Michael's family goes through many stressful days that almost destroy the family. One year later Michael has not been found.*
COMMENTS: *This story is very realistic in that it does not have a happy ending. Students learn the procedures for finding missing children and discuss how to stay safe. Many writing activities come out of this emotional book.*

DISCUSSION QUESTIONS AND WRITING EXERCISES

1. Jody looks to see if anything is missing from Michael's room. What kind of things should you look for when you search a room for clues?

2. Officer Dino tells Jody's parents that if Michael were two weeks older, or 14 years old, they would not look for him because they would automatically assume he ran away. Why?

3. After calling the police, what would you do to find a missing child?

*4. Write up a missing child flyer about Michael.

5. Michael thinks his parents are getting a divorce. Why?

6. Why do the reporters talk about Michael in the past tense?

7. After seeing how upset everyone is at Jody's house, how can Maris ask Jody if it is okay for her to run away from home? What does this tell you about Maris?

8. Jody and Jerry agree to say "David Templeton" whenever they feel like crying. What do you do in order not to cry when you feel like crying?

9. Why does Kay say she'll run away if she has to go to school?

10. Why does Kay's mom say she wishes it was Kay who was missing and not Michael? Does she mean it?

11. Jody says she'll do everything she's supposed to do when Michael comes back. Why wait?

12. Lauren says Maris is insensitive toward Jody by always talking about her petty problems with her mother. What do you think?

13. If you were Jody, would you want everyone to act as if nothing were wrong around you, or always talk about Michael? Why?

14. Why was it important that Jody and Kay go to school on the first day of the school year?

15. Jody says it is okay to hate Michael. Why?

16. Would you buy a birthday present for someone who is missing? Why?

17. Why did Jody's mom make Michael a birthday cake and expect everyone to sing "Happy Birthday"?

18. Why does Jody's mom blame her husband for Michael being missing? Whose fault do you think it is and why?

19. Why does Jody's mom blame God that Michael is missing?

20. Why does Jody's mom quit her job?

21. Why does everyone in Jody's family stop caring about anything?

22. Why do all the adults who know Jody's mom avoid her?

23. Why does no one come to Kay's party? If you had been invited, would you have gone? Why?

24. Why does Kay want to live with her grandparents? Will living with them make things better? Explain.

25. Kay tells Jody she wishes Michael were dead. Does she mean it? Is it better to know he's dead than to wonder? Explain.

*26. Kay wants to live with her grandparents where no one knows about Michael. She learns that she can't get away from Michael. Tell about a time you tried to run away from a problem.

27. Why does Jody's mother insist they all buy Christmas presents for Michael? Would you? Explain.

28. Michael has been missing for four months and life still revolves around him. How do you go about getting on with your life?

29. Jody's father believes the cops "killed" Michael by refusing to look for him that first day. Do you agree? Explain.

30. Why would the police refuse to look when the trail is the hottest?

31. Do you think the police were incompetent? Why?

*32. Who has been the best support to Jody through this, Lauren or Maris? Why?

33. Why is Kay's mother so angry with Kay for putting the ad in the paper? Do you think Kay did anything wrong? Explain.

34. Why is Kay's mother sending her away? Is she right?

35. Why is Kay's dad letting her mother make all the decisions?

*36. Pretend you are Kay. Write in your diary how you felt when your mom slapped you twice.

37. Why do the kids at school now think Jody's family has always known where Michael was?

38. Is it wrong for Kay to wish Michael were dead? Explain.

39. If you were Kay, would you ever want to go back to your family again? Why?

40. Why doesn't Kay's mother go for counseling?

41. Why does Jody think Michael is in New York City?

42. The minister tells Jody she is not responsible for saving her family. How has she been trying to?

43. Explain the statement, "Love bears all things, believes all things, endures all things. Love is never ending."

*44. Write a different ending to the story.

45. If Michael came back, what would be the first thing you would say to him?

*46. How has Jody's life changed in the last year and how will her life be different because of what she has gone through?

47. What important lesson has Jody's family learned through all of this?

RESEARCH QUESTIONS

1. How many children are reported missing each year?

2. How many missing children are found?

3. What do the police do when they first receive a missing child report?

4. What organizations are there that help locate children?

5. What support groups are available for families of missing children?

6. What can be done to help children be safe from abductors?

7. What percentage of families break up due to the stress of a missing child?

8. How long do the police look for a missing child before they give up?

9. What percentage of missing children are found murdered?

ABOUT THE AUTHORS

CHESTER AARON, English professor and writer, wanted to write ever since he read Jack London's *White Fang* at the age of eleven. Most of what Aaron writes comes from his being Jewish and having been in World War II and seen a concentration camp. Address: P.O. Box 388, Occidental, CA 95465.

VIVIEN ALCOCK, artist and writer, writes fantasy books and books with an element of the supernatural. Her books have happy endings. *The Monster Garden* won the Voice of Youth Advocate Best Science Fiction/Fantasy Book of 1988. Address: 59 Wood Lane, London N6 5UD, England.

AVI, a former librarian for 25 years, now writes full-time. As a child he had a learning disability called dysgraphia which affected his spelling and writing. His teachers never believed he would be able to become a writer. Avi proved them wrong by successfully writing many novels, several of which won awards. Avi has written many kinds of books, including but not limited to historical fiction, mystery, comedy and adventure. Avi has also illustrated books. Address: 15 Sheldon St., Providence, RI 02906.

JAY BENNETT at one time was a scriptwriter for radio and television dramas. He has won four awards for his writing, including the Edgar Allan Poe Award for *The Long Black Coat*. Bennett writes suspense mysteries. His books carry the message that you cannot make it alone—people need each other. Bennett knew he wanted to be a writer his first year in grammar school. He wrote for fourteen years before his first piece of writing was accepted. Since then he has had numerous novels and scripts published. Address: 64 Greensward, Cherry Hill, NJ 08002.

EVE BUNTING, born in Ireland, learned to write well in boarding school in Belfast. After she was married and moved to the United States, she started writing children's books. Bunting is a prolific writer and has won many awards and honors for her works. She gets her ideas from current events in the news and from what she observes. Address: 1512 Rosa Villa St., Pasadena, CA 91106.

A.E. CANNON (No information available)

GRACE CHETWIN, a teacher and career writer, writes fantasy books for young adults. She says that with fantasy one can attack social issues and ills without offending anyone. Her books all carry a message. Address: 37 Hitching Post La., Glen Cove, NY 11542.

PAM CONRAD, a career writer, is best known for her historical fiction books such as *Prairie Songs,* which has won several awards. Conrad finds some of herself in each of the books she writes. Though she began writing at an early age and wrote poetry off and on, Conrad didn't start writing seriously until after she was married. Address: c/o HarperCollins Publishers, 10 E. 53rd St., New York, NY 10022.

CAROLINE B. COONEY, who has had over 50 books published, mostly writes romance novels for teenagers, because she believes they want to read books with happy endings. Cooney wrote eight novels before her first book, *Safe as the Grave,* was published. It also was an award winner. Cooney says the best way to learn to write is to actually write. Address: c/o Curtis Brown Ltd., 10 Astor Pl. New York, NY 10003.

PAULA DANZIGER, a former reading and English teacher, lives in New York City where she works as a full-time writer. Danziger has written several books and won many awards including five for her first book, *The Cat Ate My Gymsuit.* Danziger has always wanted to be a writer and as a small child started observing her surroundings and storing events and details to use later. Most of her main characters are girls. Address: c/o Donald C. Forbes, 99 Park Ave., New York, NY 10016.

LOIS DUNCAN, a career writer, had her first article published at the age of thirteen. She began her career writing articles for magazines. Duncan is best known for her mysteries and has won numerous awards. When she was a teenager she was given the advice to write about what she knew and had experienced. This advice has served her well. Address: 1112 Dakota NE, Albuquerque, NM 87110.

CAROL FENNER, an illustrator and author, began writing and drawing as a small child. Her first poem was published by a local paper, having been submitted by her father. At age eleven she wrote plays for the neighborhood children. Address: 190 Rebecca Rd., Battle Creek, MI 49015.

JUNE FOLEY works for World Almanac and writes books with happy endings for young adults. Her characters are girls and she herself is in some way all of the leading characters. Her favorite pastime has always been reading, which got her into writing. Address: c/o Marilyn Marlow, Curtis Brown Ltd., 10 Astor Pl., New York, NY 10003.

SHERRY GARLAND, a lecturer and writer, won two awards for *Song of the Buffalo Boy.* Garland writes stories about Asia. She became interested in writing about Asians and their culture while doing volunteer work with Vietnamese families. Though she won an essay contest while in high school she didn't begin to write seriously till several years later. Address: c/o Harcourt Brace Jovanovich, 1250 Sixth Ave., San Diego, CA 92101.

MARY DOWNING HAHN is a writer, artist, and librarian. She drew pictures as a child but didn't start writing books till she was married. She prefers her books to be realistic, with her characters having strengths and weaknesses. They usually don't have happy endings. Hahn won six awards for *Daphne's Book.* Address: 9746 Basket Ring Rd., Columbia, MD 21045.

BARBARA HALL, a television screenwriter and novelist, received four citations for her young adult novel *Dixie Storms.* She started writing at the age of eight and was first published at fifteen. Hall wants her writing to be honest. She writes about kids who are forced to cope with situations that are out of their control. Address: 10720 Le Conte Ave., Los Angeles, CA 90024.

DANIEL HAYES, a teacher and writer, won the Best Book for Young Adult Citation for *The Trouble with Lemons.* Hayes decided in college to become a writer. He writes by first knowing all there is to know about his characters; then he creates a story for them. He has written two books. Address: RD No. 1, Rt. 40, Schaghticoke, NY 12154.

S.E. HINTON, a career writer, wrote her first novel, *The Outsiders,* at the age of sixteen. It was eventually made into a movie along with three of her other books. Hinton writes about teenage gangs and kids growing up poor and being the underdog. Address: c/o Delacorte Press, 1 Dag Hammarskjold Plaza, New York, NY 10017.

MONICA HUGHES, who was born in England, has lived in Egypt and the former Rhodesia and currently resides in Canada. She has won several awards for her numerous books. Hughes writes historical, realistic, and science fiction. Though she enjoyed writing as a child, it wasn't until after she married that she started her career as a writer. She got into writing science fiction because she used to be a stargazer with her father who was an amateur astronomer. She writes to help children explore the world and their future. Address: 13816 110-A Ave., Edmonton, Alberta T5M 2M9, Canada.

GORDON KORMAN began his professional writing career at the age of twelve when he wrote his first novel which was published two years later. Since then, he has averaged writing about one book a year. Korman writes slapstick humorous fiction and has his teenage characters succeed in an adults' world. He has won many awards in Canada and America for his writings and received the Air Canadian Award for being voted the Most Promising Writer Under Thirty-five. Address: 20 Dersingham Cres., Thornhill, Ontario L3T 4E7, Canada.

ROBERT LIPSYTE, a former sportswriter turned novelist, is known for his young adult novels about sports. He has also written some nonfiction books about sports. Lipsyte has won several awards for his writing, including the Child Study Association's Children's Book Award for *The Contender*. Address: c/o HarperCollins Publishers, 10 E. 53rd St., New York, NY 10022.

WALTER DEAN MYERS was raised in Harlem and writes about the good experiences he had growing up there. He writes about the black experience in Harlem to give teenagers hope. Many of his books have won awards. Address: 2543 Kennedy Blvd., Jersey City, NJ 07304.

PHYLLIS REYNOLDS NAYLOR has won numerous awards for her books. She is a prolific writer of both fiction and nonfiction, including suspense, serious, and mystery books. Address: 9910 Holmhurst Rd., Bethesda, MD 20817.

JOAN LOWERY NIXON writes mysteries, historical fiction, and adventure books for teenagers. Each genre is equally well received and loved. She has won the Edgar Allan Poe Award three times for Best Juvenile Mystery. Nixon also coauthors science books with her husband. She has written over 70 books. Address: c/o Bantam Books, 666 Fifth Ave., New York, NY 10103.

GARY PAULSEN, a career writer, has written several adventure survival books for young people. He has won several honors and awards for his work, including Newbery Honor Book in 1988 for *Hatchet* which was later made into a movie. Many of the adventures Paulsen writes about come from personal experience. He wrote *Dogsong* after competing in the Iditarod in Alaska. Paulsen travels all over the United States speaking to young people. He has a lot of faith in the youth of today. Address: c/o Ray Peekner Literary Agency, 2625 N 36th St., Milwaukee, WI 53210.

RICHARD PECK, a former English teacher and now a career writer, has written many award-winning books. His writing has been influenced by growing up listening to older folks telling stories, and many of his stories have an older, wiser character in them. Peck prefers to write novels about problems and social issues many teenagers have to deal with. Address: 155 E. 72nd St., New York, NY 10021.

SUSAN BETH PFEFFER lives in Middleton, New York where she works as a writer. She became interested in writing at the age of six when she saw her father's name on the cover of a book and her name on the dedication page. Pfeffer wrote her first story at the age of six. She has written several books and won four awards for her writing including two awards for *Kid Power*. Pfeffer grew up believing anyone could write and not just special people. Address: 14 South Railroad Ave., Middletown, NY 10940.

JILL PINKWATER (No information available.)

WILSON RAWLS is a career writer. He is best known for his award-winning book, *Where the Red Fern Grows,* which was made into a movie. The book was based on his boyhood. Rawls was taught to read and write by his mother and decided to become a writer after reading Jack London's *Call of the Wild*. Address: Rt. 2, Box 73, Cornell, WI 54732.

WILLO DAVIS ROBERTS started writing at the age of nine and since then has written over 70 books, most of which are for adults. She gets many of her story ideas and characters from her children and grandchildren, and her settings by visiting and photographing old houses. Roberts travels around the country speaking to children and working out of her motor home. Address: c/o Curtis Brown Ltd., 575 Madison Ave. New York, NY 10022.

SUSAN SHREVE is a professor of literature and a writer of novels for young adults. She has been writing since she was nine and began writing books as a teenager. Address: 3518 35th St., NW, Washington, DC 20016.

K. SMITH (No information available.)

GARY SOTO teaches at the University of California at Berkeley while he continues his writing career. Soto writes about what it is like to grow up Mexican-American. Most of his stories take place in the barrio. Though Soto has written novels, he is probably best known for his poetry which has won many awards. Soto did not grow up in a home with books and was not interested in writing until college, when he started reading poetry and thought he, too, could write it. Address: c/o Curtis Brown Ltd., 10 Astor Pl., New York, NY 10003.

JERRY SPINELLI became interested in writing at the age of sixteen, when his poem about his high school football team's victory was published in the local newspaper. His inspiration comes from watching his six children go through adolescence. Spinelli has written several books for teenagers, among which *Maniac Magee* won five awards including the Newbery Medal. Address: 331 Melvin Rd., Phoenixville, PA 19460.

MARC TALBERT, an ex-teacher turned novelist, has won several awards including some in England and Australia. He has always wanted to write and has written nine books. Address: Rt. 4, Box 1B, Santa Fe, NM 87501.

THEODORE TAYLOR, an ex-newspaper reporter and now novelist, has written numerous books and won many awards for his writings. *The Cay,* one of his best-known books, was made into a movie. Many of his books came out of his war experience and hearing Dr. Martin Luther King, Jr., speak. Address: 1856 Cataline St., Laguna Beach, CA 92615.

G. CLIFTON WISLER, an ex-journalist and teacher now career writer of novels, has written over 40 books. Wisler learned early on that he was a good storyteller. He used to tell stories around the campfire as a boy scout. Eventually some of these tales ended up in his books. Address: 1812 Savage Dr., Plano, TX 75023.

SUSAN WOJCIECHOWSKI, a former teacher now librarian and writer, writes humorous fiction. Address: 56 Reitz Pkwy., Pittsford, NY 14534.

PHYLLIS ANDERSON WOOD is an English and reading teacher who started writing novels so her students who were reluctant readers would have something interesting to read. Today her students read her manuscripts and make suggestions before the manuscripts are sent to her publisher. Address: 65 Capay Circle S., San Francisco, CA 94080.

BETTY REN WRIGHT, a career writer, has written many books and won several awards including ten for *The Dollhouse Murders.* Wright began writing poems at the age of seven and was encouraged to be a writer. She writes ghost tales and mysteries for young adults and gets many of the ideas for these books from her own life. Address: 611 47th Ave., Kenosha, WI 53144.

BIBLIOGRAPHY

Aaron, Chester. *Alex, Who Won His War.* Walker and Co., 1991, 156 pages.

Alcock, Vivien. *The Monster Garden.* Delacorte Press, 1988, 160 pages.

Avi. *The Fighting Ground.* J.B. Lippincott, 1984, 157 pages.

Bennett, Jay. *Coverup.* Watts, 1991, 144 pages.

Bennett, Jay. *The Skeleton Man.* Watts, 1986, 170 pages.

Bunting, Eve. *Is Anybody There?* J.B. Lippincott, 1988, 170 pages.

Cannon, A.E. *Shadow Brothers.* Delacorte Press, 1990, 179 pages.

Chetwin, Grace. *Collidescope.* Bradbury Press, 1990, 221 pages.

Conrad, Pam. *Prairie Songs.* Harper and Row, 1990, 130 pages.

Cooney, Caroline B. *The Face on the Milk Carton.* Bantam, 1990, 184 pages.

Cooney, Caroline B. *Flight #116 Is Down.* Scholastic, 1992, 201 pages.

Danziger, Paula. *This Place Has No Atmosphere.* Delacorte Press, 1986, 156 pages.

Duncan, Lois. *Don't Look Behind You.* Laurel Leaf/Dell, 1989, 179 pages.

Fenner, Carol. *Randall's Wall.* Margaret K. McElderry Books, 1991, 85 pages.

Foley, June. *Susanna Siegelbaum Gives Up Guys.* Scholastic, 1991, 152 pages.

Garland, Sherry. *Song of the Buffalo Boy.* Harcourt Brace, 1992, 249 pages.

Hahn, Mary Downing. *The Dead Man in Indian Creek.* Clarion Books, 1990, 130 pages.

Hahn, Mary Downing. *The Spanish Kidnapping Disaster.* Clarion Books, 1991, 132 pages.

Hall, Barbara. *Dixie Storms.* Harcourt Brace Jovanovich, 1990, 197 pages.

Hayes, Daniel. *The Trouble with Lemons.* David R. Godine, 1991, 183 pages.

Hinton, S.E. *Rumble Fish.* Delacorte Press, 1975, 122 pages.

Hughes, Monica. *Invitation to the Game.* Half Moon Books, 1992, 208 pages.

Korman, Gordon. *Losing Joe's Place.* Scholastic, 1990, 192 pages.

Lipsyte, Robert. *The Brave.* Barricade Books, 1991, 215 pages.

Lipsyte, Robert. *One Fat Summer.* Harper and Row, 1977, 152 pages.

Myers, Walter Dean. *Mouse Rap.* Harper and Row, 1990, 186 pages.

Myers, Walter Dean. *Scorpions.* Harper and Row, 1988, 216 pages.

Naylor, Phyllis Reynolds. *Alice in Rapture, Sort Of.* Atheneum, 1989, 166 pages.

Nixon, Joan Lowery. *A Candidate for Murder.* Delacorte Press, 1991, 210 pages.

Nixon, Joan Lowery. *A Family Apart.* Bantam, 1987, 162 pages.

Paulsen, Gary. *Canyons.* Delacorte Press, 1990, 184 pages.

Paulsen, Gary. *Hatchet.* Bradbury Press, 1987, 195 pages.

Paulsen, Gary. *The Island.* Orchard Books, 1988, 202 pages.

Paulsen, Gary. *The Monument.* Delacorte Press, 1991, 151 pages.

Paulsen, Gary. *The Voyage of the Frog.* Orchard Books, 1989, 141 pages.

Peck, Richard. *Are You in the House Alone?* Viking, 1976, 156 pages.

Pfeffer, Susan Beth. *The Year without Michael.* Bantam, 1987, 164 pages.

Pinkwater, Jill. *Buffalo Brenda.* Macmillan, 1989, 203 pages.

Rawls, Wilson. *Summer of the Monkeys.* Doubleday, 1976, 239 pages.

Roberts, Willo Davis. *Scared Stiff.* Atheneum, 1991, 188 pages.

Shreve, Susan. *The Gift of the Girl Who Couldn't Hear.* Tambourine Books, 1991, 79 pages.

Smith, K. *Skeeter.* Houghton Mifflin, 1989, 208 pages.

Soto, Gary. *Taking Sides.* Harcourt Brace Jovanovich, 1991, 138 pages.

Spinelli, Jerry. *There's a Girl in My Hammerlock.* Simon and Schuster, 1991, 199 pages.

Talbert, Marc. *Pillow of Clouds.* Dial Books, 1991, 204 pages.

Taylor, Theodore. *The Weirdo.* Harcourt Brace Jovanovich, 1991, 289 pages.

Wisler, G. Clifton. *The Mind Trap.* Dutton, 1990, 118 pages.

Wojciechowski, Susan. *And the Other, Gold.* Orchard Books, 1987, 151 pages.

Wood, Phyllis Anderson. *The Revolving Door Stops Here.* Cobblehill Books, 1990, 187 pages.

Wright, Betty Ren. *The Scariest Night.* Holiday House, 1991, 166 pages.

SUBJECT INDEX

DATE DUE